GROW YOUR OWN

ALEC BRISTOW

Grow Your Own

Thomas Y. Crowell, Publishers
Established 1834
New York

Created, designed and produced by
Reference International Publishers Limited.

© 1977 by Reference International
Publishers Limited.

Printed in the United States of America.

ISBN 0-690-01821-5 (Paperback)
ISBN 0-690-01803-7 (Hardcover)

LC 78-65629

Contents

1. Introduction

THIS IS A practical book. It was written to help the millions of people who want to grow food for themselves and their families but do not know how to go about it.

The numbers of those who want to grow vegetables are increasing every day, as concern becomes more widespread over the gathering crisis in the world's food supply. Nobody who opens a newspaper or listens to the radio or watches television can fail to be aware of the way in which world population is outstripping our capacity to feed ourselves; pictures of starving children in the famine-ridden areas have become so much part of our daily diet that our senses are in danger of becoming blunted. What can one do to help solve a problem of such appalling size and complexity? The answer is plenty. If every family with a garden were to turn part of it into a vegetable patch, and so provide at least some of its own food, the outlook would dramatically improve. Even people living in towns and cities, with no garden at all, should be able to rent a suitable nearby plot of ground from, say a City Parks Department, or share land with friends, neighbors or work colleagues in a community or company garden program. Even those who cannot, or do not want to, take on an outdoor vegetable garden can grow a few salads and herbs in window boxes or on window sills; and there are many seeds, such as beans, alfalfa, pumpkin, oats and fenugreek, which can be sprouted in a dark, warm place to give crisp, tasty shoots of very high food value, rich in vitamins and with a protein content of as much as forty per cent by weight.

Few people nowadays need to be told of the vital importance of protein in a healthy diet; it is indeed shortage of protein which is more than any other single factor responsible for many of the deficiency diseases that we are made so distressingly aware of in pictures from the famine-stricken areas. There was a time when it was thought that adequate amounts of protein could only be obtained from animal products, particularly meat. Now it is known that a perfectly satisfactory supply of protein can be obtained from a wholly vegetable diet. Many modern varieties which have been bred at agricultural and horticultural experiment stations over the past few years have a vastly higher protein content than would previously have been thought possible. Vegetable protein is also superior to animal protein in avoiding the build-up of cholesterol in the blood, which is thought by most specialists to be one of the main causes of heart disease, that scourge of what are laughingly called civilized societies. Add to that the fact that to produce one ton of beef it takes six tons of vegetable protein—which if it were not for our obsession with a meat diet could go a long way towards relieving malnutrition in the poor countries—and you have a formidable case for eating your protein direct from vegetable sources instead of first passing it through animals at colossal cost in money and health—not to mention the cruelty of factory farming. That is why many concerned individuals and groups are either becoming vegetarian or having 'meatless days'.

The aim of this book is not to turn you into a convert to the vegetarian cause. However, when you have experienced the much superior flavor of your own freshly gathered vegetables, have basked in the pride of achievement and have congratulated yourself on doing your bit to relieve the world food situation, you might want to become either wholly or largely vegetarian simply because it is a better way to live.

Your health should improve; certainly your personal finances should take a dramatic turn for the better, because with prices going up at an ever

Peas

faster rate all around, the best way to beat inflation is to grow your own food.

A great saving in money and at the same time improvement in both the taste and the health of your home-grown vegetables can be achieved by making use of the free supply of what at present you probably throw away. Household waste of animal and vegetable origin—scraps of leftover food, vegetable peelings, tea leaves, coffee grounds, dead flowers, even well-soaked old newspapers—will, if properly treated as explained in the chapter *Making and using compost*, provide a rich source of life-giving humus to improve and enrich your soil. No amount of chemical fertilizers will make up for a deficiency of humus; indeed, they will make matters worse in

a humus-starved soil by destroying its structure, ruining its water-holding capacity and so shrivelling the vital hair-roots of your plants. Evidence shows that in turn this makes the plants more susceptible not only to disease but to the attacks of pests, which develop a kinky taste for the highly concentrated sap of unhealthy plants. This leads to the spending of much time and effort spraying and dusting with even more chemicals to try to keep the diseases and pests under control.

We are all becoming more and more uneasy about these chemical poisons, with the slaughter of wildlife and the pollution that they bring about. The more natural your growing methods, the fewer poisons are needed.

7

2. How to use this book

A GREAT MANY books on gardening start with the assumption that the reader already knows all about the basic operations. They are the equivalent of the books on cookery that start 'Make a white sauce' without telling you how to do so.

That is reasonable enough for those who are already dedicated gardeners, have spent a good deal of time and effort on their hobby and have acquired so much practical experience that it would only be annoying to them to be taught again the elementary things they already know.

This book makes no such assumption. It is written for those who have no knowledge of the subject at all and simply want to be told the quickest, easiest and least effortful way of doing things. After all, the only sane reason for growing vegetables is so that you will get out of the operation a great deal more energy, in terms of food value, than you put into it in terms of muscle-power. If you don't get out of the ground more energy than you put into it you can't gain any satisfaction unless you are a thoroughgoing masochist; if you actually put in more energy than you get out (which unfortunately is by no means unknown) you might as well give the whole thing up.

The basic theme of the book is therefore how to get as much return as possible for as little effort as possible. That is why we start with a consideration of how much ground you can comfortably manage without becoming a slave to it and wishing pretty soon that you had never started. Then we go on to list the bare minimum of garden tools that you will need to do the job properly and after that comes an easy, step-by-step chapter on the very basic subject of how to dig, with action illustrations so that you can actually get—or at least pretend to yourself to get—real pleasure out of the operation instead of finding it a back-breaking penance.

By the same method of action pictures the other basic and essential operations are explained; improving the soil, making a compost heap (so that every scrap of suitable household waste is returned to the soil, to make things grow instead of merely adding to waste and pollution), raking, sowing and planting and thinning.

The chapter on fertilizers and manures puts the argument for and against the artificial chemicals that some say are vital to soil productivity but others say damage the structure of the land, poison not only beneficial soil organisms but the roots of crops, spoil the taste of the produce and increase attacks by pests and diseases.

Chapters follow on the individual vegetable crops that can be grown in your patch, when to sow and harvest and—vital but controversial—how to deal with the ills that afflict them. Once again, opinion is divided on this subject. There are those who swear by the latest fungicides and pesticides and assert that we cannot get worthwhile crops without them. On the other hand there are others who—with a mounting body of evidence to support them—say that these expensive, complex and mostly evil-smelling chemicals should never be used: they are dangerous to human beings, they poison wild life, they ruin the soil, they murder the beneficial predatory creatures which, if allowed to live, would themselves kill and eat the insect pests. What is worse, they are in many cases becoming ineffective because new races of superpests are making their appearance which have not only developed resistance to, but indeed seem to thrive on, these modern chemicals. As a result, ever more powerful and dangerous chemicals are continually emerging from the laboratories and the situation has become so alarming that many of these chemicals are now being banned by government authorities in some places and more authorities are bound to follow suit to try to avert possible disasters. Because of the difficulties and dangers of these modern pesticides, no recommendations are made on their use. Where possible, older methods of control are given; some of them may not be one hundred per cent efficient, some may be nothing but old wives' tales, but at least even if they don't kill all the pests they are not likely to kill birds, pets or human beings either.

However, many modern varieties of vegetables are very much better than the old-fashioned ones, both in yield—which in many cases may be three or four times as much as those of ten years ago—and in resistance to diseases and pests which has been bred into them by the modern plant breeders, sometimes making use of natural species to cross with garden varieties of delicate constitution so as to re-introduce the robust resistance that nature had evolved over the centuries. Where these modern varieties of proved performance are available, reference to them is made under the different vegetables dealt with throughout the book.

Plant breeders are producing so many excellent new varieties at horticultural stations throughout the world, that it is always possible that your dealer has something new to offer that is worth a trial. In particular, look for the new F1 hybrids that are created as the first-generation offspring of selected varieties. These can be relied on to be more robust, tastier and better looking than their parents.

Snap beans, pole variety

3. How much ground?

BEFORE GOING any further, we had better decide how big your vegetable patch is going to be.

How much ground can you manage to the best advantage? If you are an ordinary person the answer will be about 500 to 600 square yards (c. 500 m²) at the most. By an ordinary person I mean one who works all day and has only a limited amount of time and energy left over for growing vegetables.

Some enthusiasts suggest that a fair-sized patch would be nearer 1,000 square yards (1,000 m²); like most enthusiasts they are too obsessed to think about the needs of ordinary people. To zealots, no doubt, the growing of vegetables is the most beautiful occupation in the world. The average person wants to tackle the smallest area that will give satisfactory results.

So if you are an ordinary hard-working person, confine yourself to 600 square yards at the most, similar to the area shown as *A* plus *B* in the photograph. That should produce enough vegetables for an average family all the year; it might even produce a surplus for sale. To look after this plot properly will take about five hours a week most of the year, rising perhaps to seven or eight hours a week in the busy season (spring) and dropping to two or three hours in the winter. If that seems too much, and you have only a small family to feed, you can manage quite well with a plot half that size, as in the area marked *A* in the photograph. Look at it. If it seems to be what you can manage, settle for that. It should, if well cultivated and productive, produce quite enough vegetables for two or three people.

Whatever you do, don't take on a larger piece of ground than you can manage comfortably. Take a look at the total area *A* plus *B* plus *C* in the photograph and see if it makes you feel tired out just to look at it. It is over 1,000 square yards. This may not sound possible, but it is a well established fact that if you try to tackle a patch this size and cannot give it the time and labor it demands you will

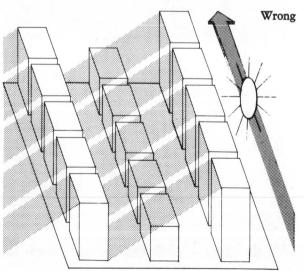

Wrong

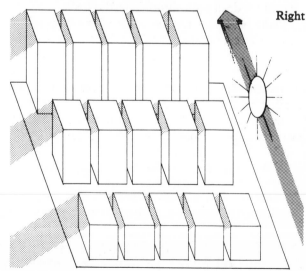

Right

The size of the plot

actually get less out of it than you would from a plot half the size that you can look after well.

Which way should your vegetable patch face? Most people, I suppose, will have to take whatever site there is available, but if you have any choice in the matter, pick out a plot that is entirely open, not shaded by trees; particularly it should have no obstruction which might cause shade to the south. If the patch is oblong, which it should be, choose one such as is shown here, with the long side running east and west. Then the rows of vegetables will run north and south—which, as you can see, means they

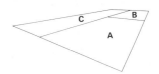

will get the sun all day long.

The type of soil that your ground is composed of is also a matter that you are unlikely to be able to choose. Good medium loam is best, but there is almost no soil that cannot be made fertile by correct treatment.

4. The tools you need

THE following implements are indispensable:

Spade   Hoe
Spading Fork   Watering Can
Rake   Garden Line

That is all. With the six tools listed above you can work a garden plot perfectly well. Of course, there are other implements that can make useful additions, such as the Dutch scuffle hoe, which is a great help with weeds during the summer (though there are some now who would say, on the evidence of recent investigation, that it is a pernicious instrument which does more harm by damaging roots than good by chopping up weeds). And no doubt when you are buying the tools the salesman will suggest all kinds of extra gadgets to lighten your labor. The snag, in my experience, is that some of these new labor-saving gadgets are not only much more expensive than the good old-fashioned tools but create more labor than they save.

Here are some hints to help you choose the best tools for your purpose.

SPADE   You are going to use this a great deal, so be careful to choose a good one. It should be chosen for the same qualities as for a good friend—that is, it should be bright, well balanced and of good temper, like the one shown here. If you can afford a stainless steel one, it will be a joy to use, because even the heaviest soil does not cling to it in the same way that it tends to do with a non-stainless one.

If you cannot afford the stainless type, which is almost self-cleaning, you will need a scraper (wooden or metal) which, with a loop of string, can be carried over your shoulder ready to be used as you go along in order to remove any clinging lumps of earth from the blade that would clog it and prevent it from cutting cleanly through the soil. The important

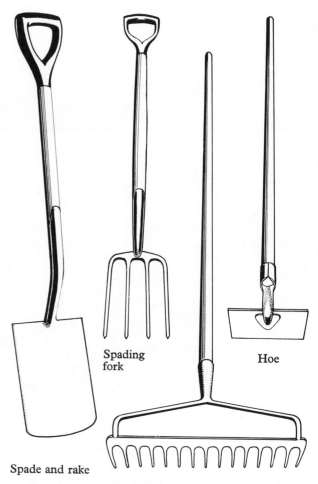

Spading fork

Hoe

Spade and rake

thing is that the center of gravity should be only five or six inches above the point where the blade of the spade meets the shaft. That is to say, if you hold the shaft lightly between your thumb and fingers just above the blade the spade should lie horizontal, without overbalancing towards one end or the other. This correct balance makes all the difference between effortless digging and hard labor.

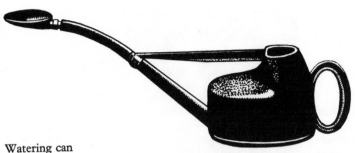

Watering can

Garden line

SPADING FORK The fork shown in the drawing is also a stainless steel one. Once again, this makes for smoother and easier digging, but the advantage is not so marked as with a spade, because the earth hasn't got the same amount of surface to cling to. The center of gravity should be in a similar position to that of the spade (see above).

RAKE The best for your purpose is a steel bow one with at least twelve teeth, which should be rigid; the flexible kind, admirable for lawns, is no use for raking soil.

HOE There are several kinds of hoe—some very new and gimmicky—but the best type for what you want (which includes the earthing up of potatoes) has a 6-inch wide blade.

WATERING CAN A 2-gallon plastic one will be serviceable. It should have a detachable rose head nozzle, or better still two roses, one coarse and one fine.

GARDEN LINE The one pictured here is a wrought-iron affair with a revolving winder, the other end of the line being tied to an iron pin. Or it may be simply two sticks with the line wound upon one of them. In either case, it is a good idea to choose a

nylon twine for the line itself; this will be more expensive at first, but it will last almost for ever.

WHEELBARROW In addition to these indispensables, you should, if it is humanly possible, have a wheelbarrow. One of the modern lightweight ones, such as that shown here, is an excellent buy, especially if it is the low-slung type which can be tilted down to ground level so that things do not have to be lifted either to load or to unload it.

Wheelbarrow

5. How to dig

Let's face it—the first thing you must do with your vegetable patch is to dig it, even if later on you decide to have a try at one of the 'no dig' systems (of which more in a later chapter). Before you can plant, or sow, or do anything else, that patch of ground must be dug.

But don't let it frighten you. There is not the slightest reason why digging should wear you out, break your back, or make you stiff for days afterwards. As a matter of fact, when you have learned to dig correctly you might even find yourself liking it in a perverse sort of way.

Before you can begin you must be sure that the ground is workable—that is, neither soggy wet nor bone-dry—and that your spade is clean and bright.

Most beginners, as soon as they find themselves faced with the job of digging, form an enlarged opinion of their own strength and capabilities. They take enormously thick spadefuls that would daunt even an experienced gardener and then wonder why they get tired out so easily. Perhaps they have some misguided idea that by doubling the thickness of each clod of earth they will halve the number of rows they have to dig. So they turn what might have been pleasant exercise into penal servitude, because *two thin rows are much quicker to do than one thick row*.

There are five different movements in handling a spade properly, as pictured here.

Get into the habit of thinking of each spadeful of earth you dig not as a lump but as a *slice*. And cut each slice, at least to start with, thinner than you would like. Even a thoroughly experienced worker who has been digging for years would not attempt to take a slice more than 8 inches (20 cm.) thick, so keep yourself to a thickness of only 4 or 5 inches (10 or 12 cm.). Later, when your muscles have become used to the work, you might manage

First
Take the upper end of the handle with the right hand, palm towards you. Hold the lower part of the shaft lightly with the left hand. Lift the spade vertically and bend your elbows until your left forearm is horizontal.

14

6 inches (15 cm.).

The technical name for these slices of earth is 'spits', a spit being taken the full depth of the spade. So ground that has been dug to the depth of the spade in this way is said to have been dug 'one spit deep'. The first rule of digging without back-ache, then, is to take thin slices, or 'spits'. But at least as important as this is the correct handling of your spade. Many amateurs, when they get a spade in their hands, forget they own a body. They suddenly become all arms and legs—mostly arms. Instead of letting the weight of their body do nearly all the work for them, they strain their muscles almost to breaking-point by lifting each spadeful of earth as high as they can and then throwing it to the ground again.

If you stop and think you will see that it is simply a waste of energy to lift something up and then throw it down again. Lifting soon wears you out because of the strain it places on the muscles of your arms and chest. If persisted in, lifting can become positively dangerous, by putting a severe strain on your heart.

So you should look upon the digging of a piece of ground not as *lifting* it but simply as *turning it over*. There is all the difference in the world between the two processes. In lifting, the right hand holds the lower end of the shaft and does all the work.

Second
Bring the spade vertically downwards, letting the shaft slide easily through the fingers of the left hand. As soon as the edge of the blade begins to enter the soil, put your left foot on the left shoulder of the spade.

Third
Throw the whole weight of your body on to the spade and drive it in to its full depth. You will find at the finish of this movement that both your hands are at the top end of the handle, the left hand just below the right.

Fourth
Remove your left foot from the spade and pull down with the left hand in its original position until the end of the handle almost touches the ground. This will lever the 'spit' right off the ground.

Fifth
Sway forward with the whole body giving a slight twist with both wrists. Done correctly, this will turn the slice of earth over and throw it forward a little, so as to leave a narrow trench.

Palm upwards, it lifts the whole weight of the earth, without any help from either the other hand or the body.

The correct method of digging is exactly the opposite. Palm *downwards*, the left hand loosely grasps the lower end of the shaft. The right hand, with the whole weight of the body behind it, pushes the top end of the handle down towards the ground, so levering up the spadeful with very little effort.

All the movements shown here are for a right-handed person. If you are left handed, reverse your position, as in this photograph, throughout the whole sequence of operations. Better still, if you can manage it, dig one row right-handed and the next left-handed, and so on to the end of the piece of ground. This will lighten your task still further, by shifting the work from one set of muscles to another in alternate rows. As you can see, when the spade has been emptied of its load of soil at the end of movement 5, you will find that your hands are correctly placed to lift it into the first position again, ready to cut another spit. Firmly resist the impulse to pat down the spadeful of earth you have just turned over. Not only is this a waste of energy but it is actually harmful to the soil. A piece of ground may look nice flattened down, but you are not digging for the look of the thing, and anyway the weather will do the job of levelling much better than you can.

If the ground is dug, as it should be, in the fall, the rough surface will allow frost to penetrate quite deeply, so that the soil is frozen several times during the winter and each time the lumps become broken down more and more thoroughly. By the time the soil is due to be raked in the spring it will crumble into a much finer surface than could ever be achieved without nature's help. Never try to do by human effort what nature will do better.

Left-handed digging

6. Improving the soil

THE SOIL of your vegetable patch almost certainly needs improving in one way or another—probably in several ways at once.

To take the most difficult conditions first, let us suppose that you are starting with a piece of rough, uncultivated ground, covered with coarse grass and strong-rooted perennial weeds such as nettles or thistles. It is hard to dig the ground at all, even though you are armed with energy, enthusiasm, a bright new spade and all the good advice given in the last section.

The most sensible thing is to remove the surface completely. Starting at one end of the plot, skim off the vegetation, as shown. The easiest way is to cut it into oblong pieces of turf, each 1 inch thick and the width and length of the blade of the spade. Slice off a strip two turfs wide and either the full width or half the width of the plot according to how you are going to deal with it.

If there is an odd corner of ground to spare, you can make the turf into useful loam by piling it into a stack. Simply place the turfs in layers, grass

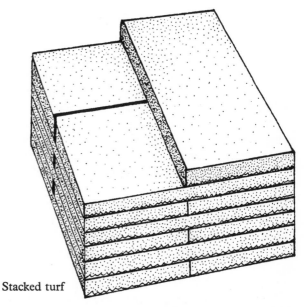

Stacked turf

side downwards, so that they die and rot down into a rich fibrous material, full of goodness, which can be added to the soil next year to improve its texture and increase its fertility. To speed up the rotting down process you can sprinkle each layer of turf with ammonium sulphate (or, if the soil is acid, alternate layers with lime). If making a loam stack in this way, remove the turfs in strips the full width of the plot and continue along the plot until it is completely bare.

Even if your ground is not in such a rough state and does not need the surface removed, it will still need improving. Good vegetable-growing soil is very rarely natural, but the result of hard work and loving care.

What *is* good soil? Looking at that patch of ground that has to be dug, you may be tempted to say that good soil is simply easily-worked soil. But that is not even half the story. True, easy working is very

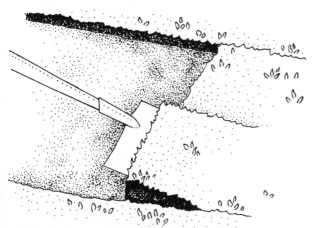

Turf removal

desirable, but there is much more to good soil than that. After all, pure sand would be very easy to work indeed, but useless for growing worthwhile crops.

Plants cannot grow without food, so it is important that your soil should contain enough of the right foods to make for healthy growth. Of these the most important are the following three elements: nitrogen, phosphorus and potassium. Nearly all the food value of almost any manure or fertilizer consists of one or more of those elements. (There are, in fact, several others—usually called 'trace elements'— that plants also need in very small quantities, but it is so rare to find any ordinary soil seriously lacking in them that we can safely ignore them.)

It is useless, then, to try to grow vegetables in soil deficient in nitrogen, phosphorus or potassium. But that does not mean that you will necessarily have to spend money straight away on manures or fertilizers. If your patch of ground has not been used for growing vegetables before, it will most likely contain quite enough food to last for the first year or two. So, as you want to know what to do here and now, we will not bother with added plant-foods until the later section on *Manures and fertilizers*. Your first efforts at soil improvement should be directed therefore not at giving your vegetables extra food but at helping them to digest what is already available. Vegetables, like new-born babies, cannot eat solid food; they can only drink, and they can take only very diluted solutions; anything stronger would kill them. So their liquid diet has to be prepared for them. This pre-digestion is done in the soil by tiny microbes, or bacteria, which spend their lives breaking down complex substances in the earth into simple forms that are easily assimilated by plant roots. Good earth teems with millions of these bacteria, so your efforts should aim

at multiplying the number in your vegetable patch. To form the right breeding ground for them, soil should be airy, deep and damp (but not soaking wet). Should your ground fall short of those requirements, the bacteria will not thrive; nor will your vegetables, which will suffer both in quality and in quantity. This is sure to happen if your soil is too heavy, too light or too shallow. Fortunately, these defects are easily recognized when you start digging.

Too HEAVY soil is difficult to dig even in good weather, but in wet weather it becomes impossible, clinging to your spade and boots and becoming more like a quagmire with every step you take. In dry weather it is equally difficult to dig because it becomes as hard as rock. Rain water cannot drain away in heavy soil but stays in the ground, chilling— or even rotting—the roots of the vegetables and drowning the useful bacteria. Even in dry weather nothing can breathe properly in heavy soil.

Too LIGHT soil is usually light in color as well as texture, and generally sandy. It is so easy to dig that it seems too good to be true. Unfortunately, however easy it is, it has one great defect. It cannot hold water. In hot weather it becomes bone dry and the roots of the vegetables shrivel from lack of moisture. It often lacks plant foods, but even if it contains enough they cannot be assimilated without water. Besides, bacteria must have moisture too; drought kills them as effectively as floods.

Too SHALLOW soil may be quite all right at the surface, but it does not readily dig to a full spade's depth. At 4 or 5 inches down, the spade hits hard subsoil, and it is almost impossible to drive it any farther. Obviously vegetables cannot send their roots far enough down in such soil to enable them to grow well.

To deal with the worst condition first, what can be done with soil that is so heavy that it remains waterlogged whatever you do? The only really satisfactory way is to drain it. At intervals across the plot trenches are dug at least 2 feet (c. 60 cm.) deep, and earthenware drainpipes are laid at the bottom. If possible these drains should lead to a deep soakaway filled with large stones, bricks or builder's rubble; better still, if there is a nearby ditch they should lead into that. Over the drainpipes lay 2 or 3 inches (c. 5–8 cm.) of coarse gravel, over that a single layer of turf, and over that the subsoil and the topsoil, replaced in the correct order. Apart from such extreme cases, all three soil defects—too heavy, too light or too shallow—can be remedied in the same ways.

1. Double digging

This means digging the ground to a depth of two spits, and so breaking up the subsoil. With heavy soil this will get rid of surplus water, so warming up the soil and letting in some air. With light soil it will enable the roots to go deeper for their water in dry weather. With shallow soil it will have the obvious effect of making it deeper. It may seem an arduous job to dig a piece of ground two spades deep, but it is not too bad if you go about it the following way:

Stretch your garden line across the plot at a distance of 2 feet from the end at which you intend to start. Remove all the topsoil from this, to the full depth of your spade, as far as half-way across the plot (strip 1 in the illustration) and pile this soil beside the other half, as shown. You now have a

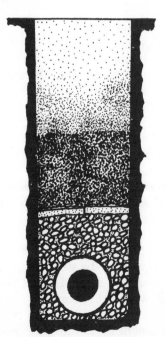

Draining

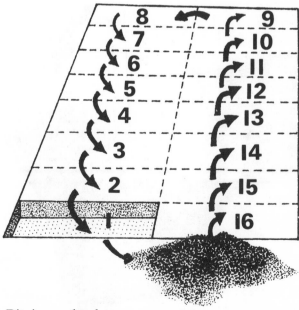

Digging up the plot

trench 2 feet wide running half-way across the plot. Get into this trench and dig the subsoil to the depth of another spit, using your fork for this operation. It is not necessary to turn the subsoil over; you only need to break it up to the full depth of the fork.

Now move your garden line back another 2 feet and dig out another trench to the half-way mark (strip 2 in the illustration). Throw the topsoil from this forward into trench 1 so as to cover the subsoil you have just broken up.

Next break up the subsoil in trench 2 with the fork. Cover this with the topsoil from strip 3 and continue in this way to the end of the plot. Fill in trench 8 with the topsoil from strip 9 on the other side of the plot, break up the subsoil, cover with topsoil from strip 10 and continue back along the second half in this way. The pile of topsoil from trench 1, which was put on one side at the beginning of the operation, is in just the right position to fill in the final trench, at strip 16, with the least possible effort.

If you did not completely strip the turf from your patch of ground and use it to make a loam-stack, as shown earlier, you can deal with it very easily during the course of double-digging. Simply start by skimming the turf from strip 1 to half way across the plot and piling it at the side. Dig out the rest of the topsoil from strip 1 and pile this separately from the turf. Then skim the turf from strip 2 and chop it up into trench 1 before covering it with the topsoil from strip 2. Continue in this way along the plot and back again. The chopped-up turf, which now forms a layer between the topsoil and the subsoil, will rot down and enrich the ground.

2. Addition of humus

The second way to improve your soil is by the addition of humus—that is, decayed vegetable matter. Humus is what makes the soil of vegetable gardens that have been worked for many years into that dark, rich material which is fibrous, and crumbly, and grows the best crops.

Apart from the valuable plant food it contains, humus lightens heavy ground and makes it easier to dig, while it enriches shallow soil, and helps light soil to hold moisture. Bacteria love humus. It is warm and airy, allowing them to breathe, and it remains damp without ever getting sticky.

We have already added a certain amount of humus to the ground during the process of turning over the soil, whether by single-digging or double-digging, because of the grass and weeds that we have buried, which will decay and enrich the earth. But we need all the humus we can get, and for this reason you should never throw away any vegetable

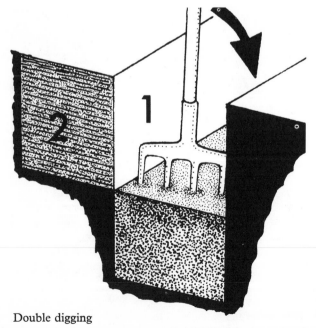

Double digging

matter—dead leaves, lawn clippings, even tea leaves and coffee grounds—but turn them into compost, as described in the section *Making and using compost*.

An excellent way of adding humus to the soil is by means of animal manure from farmyard or stables. Unfortunately it is rather scarce and expensive in these days of mechanization but it has the great advantage over all artificial fertilizers (which are only chemicals) that it contains humus. In fact, it is practically all humus. So if you can get farmyard or stable manure you will find it of the greatest value in improving your soil.

Manure, especially if it contains a good deal of straw, should be well rotted before being added to the soil. It must never be buried in a solid layer, or it might become poisonous to plant roots. Manure only does its work properly when it is well mixed with the earth, so the best way to apply it is to fork it in during digging operations.

In the section *Rotation of crops*, and in sections on particular vegetables, you will find that certain plants should never be grown in freshly manured ground.

So much for the physical properties of animal manures in improving the soil. Their value as plant food is dealt with later in the section *Manures and fertilizers*.

3. Ridging

In the section *How to dig* it was pointed out that newly dug ground should never be patted down neatly but should be left rough, so that the weather can get at it. Frost and ice pulverize the soil and improve its condition much more successfully, and with much less effort, than human labor. With really heavy soil, nature can be helped in its work if the ground is ridged during digging. As shown in

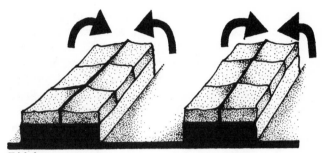

Ridging

the illustration, this is a very simple operation. The ground is divided into strips, 2 spades wide. Alternate strips are dug out, the topsoil being piled right and left on to the other strips, where it is left in clods which will crumble during the winter frosts so that they rake down into a fine surface ready for sowing in the spring.

7. Labor-saving devices

WE HAVE already seen, in the section of this book called *The tools you need*, that you can manage an average vegetable patch perfectly well with a few basic tools. However, if you want to save yourself some of the physical effort involved in such operations as digging, sowing, planting and weeding, there are hundreds of labor-saving devices which can be bought at most garden stores. The salesman will be delighted to show them to you—especially the most expensive ones—and to tell you how they will practically do the job for you, with no work at all on your part. Don't believe every word he says. Nothing can be done without any effort. Besides, if one of the reasons why you have decided to grow your own vegetables is to save money, it would not make much sense to spend such a lot on equipment that it would take several years' crops to pay it back.

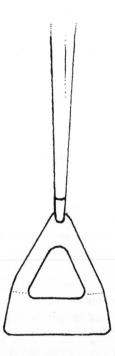

Dutch scuffle hoe

Whatever else you may want, or need, the simple and venerable hoe is essential for vegetable growing. It is used for several operations, such as making seed drills, chopping out weeds and earthing up potatoes and celery. Many gardeners also use it for keeping the surface of the ground loose. This is done for several reasons: first to destroy weeds between rows while they are still tiny seedlings, before they get a chance to grow into vigorous plants which choke your young vegetables and prevent them from getting either the air or the food they need. Weeds have their uses, as we shall see in the section on *Making and using compost*, but they must never be allowed to compete with your vegetables because, being native to your soil, they start off with unfair advantages and are bound to win any such competition.

The second reason for keeping the surface of the soil loose is to allow air to get in; this is important for strong root growth, since roots cannot take up food and water properly without air. The third reason is to let in rain. If the surface of the ground gets baked hard during dry weather, a welcome shower of rain can be quite wasted, because instead of sinking into the soil where it can be absorbed by the roots of your crops it either runs off the surface or evaporates in the sun.

The fourth reason for hoeing the surface is to keep moisture in the soil even when there is no rain. Some people maintain that if the ground is always kept hoed there is hardly ever any need to water plants.

In a hot dry summer the difference between crops on hoed and non-hoed ground can be quite remarkable. The trouble with soil that has not been hoed is that it tends to bake hard; as it does so it shrinks and then deep cracks appear, through which what little moisture is left in the ground evaporates.

By keeping the surface loose, the hoe prevents this hardening and cracking of the ground and so stops evaporation. So it is a wicked waste of all the work you have put into your vegetable patch if you skimp the business of hoeing. It is in any case quite a soothing occupation if properly done, and not at all laborious; besides, if you don't do it you may well face the much more laborious task of watering your plants to prevent them from shrivelling up— that is unless the drought is so severe that you are not allowed to water anyway.

The basic nurseryman's hoe is used with a chopping movement towards you. Do not chop *downwards*. The blade is not intended to go deep, but merely to loosen the surface; therefore it should enter the ground horizontally rather than vertically. Take the lower part of the handle in your right hand and the upper part in your left hand, keeping both palms downwards. Chop lightly so that the blade just skims below the surface and loosens it. When using this hoe you walk forwards. You can easily avoid treading on the surface if you walk in the next row to the one you are doing. The Dutch scuffle hoe pictured here is used in exactly the opposite way, which many people find so much less effortful that they would consider it well worth the extra cost of buying one in addition to the basic hoe. Instead of chopping towards you, you push the tool away from you; this makes it easier to skim the blade along just beneath the surface because you can use the push-hoe in an almost horizontal position. It is practically impossible to mess up the surface of the ground with this implement. A good one is a real pleasure to use because it is so light to handle, especially between rows of seedlings. Although you push it forward, you walk backwards when using it, so be very careful that you do not tread on any plants.

Shown next is the narrow type of push-hoe that

many people find easier still to use. It is quite a bit narrower than the traditional kind, and good for performing light jobs in narrow places.

Another modern design that is particularly good for heavy soil makes use of the fact that it is much easier to stick a point into a hard surface than a straight edge, however sharp. So the blade has teeth on both the front and the back edges, enabling it to be pushed and pulled just below the surface of the ground. This pattern is excellent if there are many stones about.

Although most of your vegetables will be sown where they are to grow, some will need to be transplanted. It is perfectly satisfactory to make the planting holes with a blunt pointed stick so long as its diameter is big enough for the roots to be spread out instead of squashed together; a broken wooden spade handle, or even broom handle, with its end rounded off is quite good enough.

Every year more elaborate and expensive new gadgets appear in the gardening stores, alleged to make the process of planting easier than it has ever been before. Beware of such things, however attractive they may look in their bright new package, or you may find yourself the owner of yet one more piece of equipment that you will try once, find that it does not make your life easier, in spite of what the advertisement says, and never use it again.

However, the whole planting operation is made easier and pleasanter if you have a trowel and a hand fork, like the pair shown here. Ones made of ordinary steel are more than adequate, but stainless steel ones, though much more expensive, are a joy to use; perhaps you can persuade someone to buy you a pair for your birthday. Among genuine labor-saving devices are some designed to break down stub-

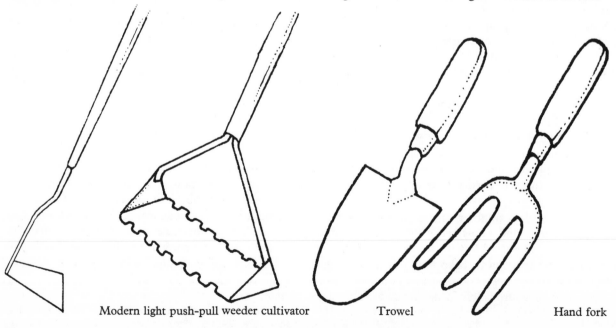

Modern light push-pull weeder cultivator   Trowel   Hand fork

born ground which resists most attempts to produce a surface where it is possible to sow or plant with any chance that the young seedlings will survive. Such devices are of two kinds: those that rely entirely on human energy and those that are powered by some form of motor. Before buying any equipment of this kind, ask if you may take it home and see if you can manage it in the real-life conditions of your vegetable plot; it may seem fine in the showroom, but only you can tell whether it will be suitable for your purpose. For really difficult soil, especially if you were not able to dig it until the spring so that it missed the beneficial action of the winter frosts, there is a whole armory of rather fearsome-looking clawed tools called cultivators that enable you to break down the soil without too much exertion. The simple three-pronged one shown here will successfully tackle quite large lumps

of earth so long as they are not too dry or too wet. For breaking down very large and stubborn clods of earth there are heavier and more formidable cultivators such as this five-pronged one. It has the advantage of being adjustable so that some of the prongs may be taken out if you do not want to use them all. By simply undoing the thumbscrew and removing the unwanted claws, you can turn the implement into a three-pronged, a two-pronged, or even a one-pronged affair. In this way you can use it not only to break down difficult soil but to cultivate with great precision, and in one operation, between rows of vegetables set at different distances apart. However, you will probably find that for most of the time you make use of it with all its prongs in place, so it is necessary to take the implement to pieces occasionally and grease the prongs where they fit into the slot, so that they remain easily detachable.

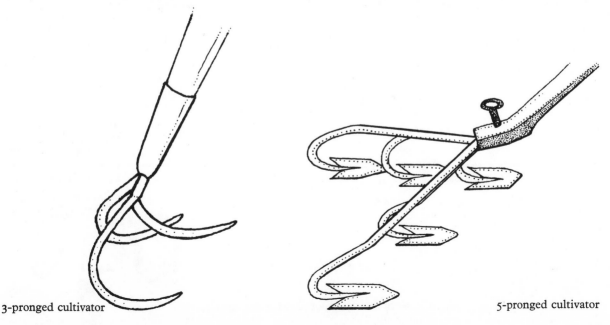

3-pronged cultivator

5-pronged cultivator

If you have taken on a large vegetable plot and find that even those pronged cultivators need too much muscle-power, there are wheeled ones such as that shown here which require less effort still, because the weight is entirely borne by the wheels and all you have to do is to push.

However, this sort of thing is more expensive still, needs to be housed in a rain-proof place to prevent it from rusting, and is not very efficient except on fairly even ground; if it has to be used on really rough land with a very uneven surface it can be more trouble than it is worth.

If your vegetable plot is even larger, so that you do not think you can conquer it by your own unaided muscle-power, the last word in implements—and unfortunately in expense—is a mechanized rotary tiller, powered by a gasoline motor, such as the one shown here. The basic mechanism is a set of blades, like a series of hoes, which are driven round and

round and eat their way into the soil as you walk along behind the machine guiding it by means of the handlebars. In this way the digging is done for you without any effort on your part, and the depth to which the soil is stirred depends upon the angle at which you hold the handlebars; the lower you hold them, the shallower the cultivation, and the more you push them forward the deeper the blades bite into the soil. At first you feel that the machine is the master, dragging you after it like a large unruly dog, but you soon learn to control it. Most of these rotary hoes have a range of different attachments to enable you to perform all the usual operations of soil cultivation mechanically. They are wonderful for breaking up a large piece of rough ground quickly, but they have one serious snag, apart from the cost of buying and maintaining them; they chop up and scatter the roots of perennial weeds such as thistles, quackgrass and bindweed, so that you may

2-wheeled cultivator   Mechanized tiller

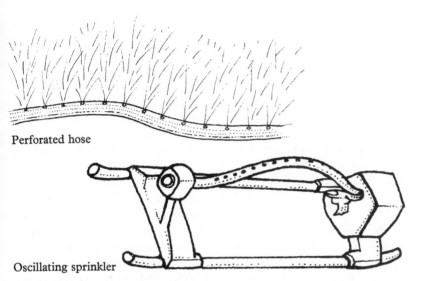

Perforated hose

Oscillating sprinkler

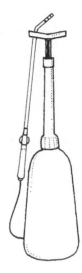

Plastic sprayer

well finish up with ten times as many such weeds as you started with.

During dry weather you may need to water some of your shallower-rooted vegetables to stop them wilting. Doing so with a watering can is a very arm-aching and backstraining operation. So long as the drought is not so severe that you are forbidden by law to use a hose, a simple and cheap watering device is a length of flat hose like the one shown here, which is perforated at intervals and gives a fine mist-like spray to quite a distance on each side. Or there are oscillating sprinklers such as the one illustrated which move from side to side and so will water a rectangular patch. This is much better than the revolving type of sprinkler which waters a circular area of ground. The result is that some parts are left without water at all, while other parts get a double soaking, which cannot possibly be avoided, from overlapping circles of spray. With the oscillating sprinkler this problem does not arise, since it is quite easy when moving it from place to place to make sure

that there is no overlap.

To fight pests and diseases you need some sort of sprayer. The simplest is a syringe which is filled from a bucket, but its use can be quite tiring. The most effortless sprayer is a lightweight plastic container like the one pictured, which is pumped up before you start spraying and makes the job much quicker and pleasanter.

The great advantage of this kind of pneumatic sprayer is that you do not have to pump it continuously in use. You therefore have both hands free. One hand can direct the spray where it is needed while the other can turn back leaves to enable the spray to reach the underside. This is extremely important, since it is the undersurface of leaves that is much more vulnerable to attack by pests and diseases than the upper side, which is protected by a tougher skin. The underside of a leaf contains the pores, which are open to attack, so that is the part that should always be thoroughly wetted by the spray.

8. Making and using compost

THESE DAYS it is not very easy to get the good, steamy, smelly old-fashioned farmyard and stable manures that before the age of machinery used to be the way our ancestors put back into the soil the goodness that the crops they grew took out of it. But it was not only the plant foods that these animal manures supplied. Because the dung was mixed with straw and other bulky material it kept the soil in good heart, as gardeners say, by putting fibrous material into it which improved its texture, helped it to drain but at the same time kept the moisture in, and warmed it up. Like human beings, plant roots need not only food but a comfortable environment if they are to be healthy and happy. Again like human beings, they cannot thrive on chemicals alone, but need bulk in their diet if they are to digest their food properly and eliminate poisons from their system.

What then are we to do if we cannot find a supply of animal manure or if it is so expensive that we cannot afford it?

The answer lies in the compost heap. Every garden should have one. Its purpose is to make use of every scrap of kitchen and garden waste, which would otherwise be thrown away, and turn it into the rich, nourishing material that vegetables need for sturdy growth. A wooden bin such as the one shown here is ideal for compost-making. It consists of four posts sunk into the ground (embedded in concrete for preference, to keep them upright and prevent them from rotting) and planks of wood nailed to them on three sides of the bin. Use galvanized nails for this; ordinary iron ones will quickly rust. Plenty of room is left between planks so that air can get into the compost and keep it sweet; without air the compost may turn into a thick, slimy mess.

The planks at the front of the bin are not fixed but can slide in and out; this is so that they can be removed to allow compost material to be added to the heap and to let the finished produce be shovelled out when it is ready for use. The drawing of a corner of the bin shows how this may be done. An upright board is nailed to the post with wooden spacing-pieces between. This makes slots which, if they are deeper and wider than the planks which are to go into them, will allow them to slide in and out easily.

There is almost no vegetable waste that cannot be used to make compost. Vegetable trimmings from the kitchen, potato peelings, discarded leaves, coffee grounds, tea leaves, whatever comes to hand. With this can be mixed grass mowings, fallen leaves from trees, straw and even old newspaper, which is made from wood pulp and so is perfectly good vegetable matter.

Many people say that diseased plants should never be put on the compost heap, because there is a danger of spreading the disease with the compost. But if the heap has been made properly, so that it develops a high temperature, the disease germs will

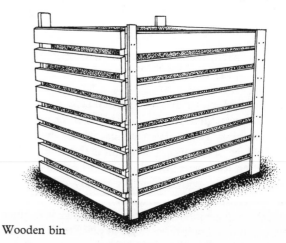

Wooden bin

have been successfully killed, so that the danger does not arise.

What creates the heat is the activity of millions and millions of bacteria and other micro-organisms whose natural function it is to break down waste material and turn it into simple substances which in their turn are used by growing plants, so that decay leads to growth and growth to decay and then to growth again in an alternating cycle that keeps life going. The tremendous amount of energy released by the bacteria makes heat, and the heat makes vegetable matter decay quicker, so that the transformation of the waste material into compost is speeded up. Another good reason why heat is so valuable is that although it encourages friendly microbes to increase and multiply it spells death to soil pests, which it cooks, and it destroys most of the things that cause plant diseases. It also kills any weed seeds that happen to have got into the compost.

In addition to air and heat, the beneficial bacteria need moisture, so if the compost heap can be sited in a shady spot where the sun is unlikely to dry it out, so much the better. If you only have a small amount of material to compost, you can buy a ready-made wire mesh container with hinged sides, as shown. It will not last for ever, but should do so for several years, during which it will much more than pay for itself by producing a good quantity of useful compost.

A modern type of compost bin is the circular one pictured next. It is made up of sections that slot into each other, and one of the sections can easily be slid up so that the finished compost can be dug out from the bottom. A plastic top can be put over the surface of the compost in bins such as this so that it never dries out and so needs no watering.

Many people nowadays put sheets of heavy-gauge black plastic over their compost heaps, whether in bins or in the open, to keep in the heat and the moisture. These act very well so long as there is enough ventilation at the sides; if the compost is not allowed any air it will soon turn into a solid, slimy, revolting mess that will do the soil more harm than good. Hedge trimmings may be used so long as they are soft and not too woody. Really hard woody branches and prunings would take too

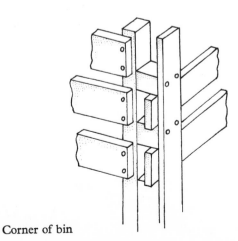

Corner of bin

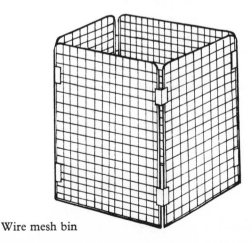

Wire mesh bin

long to rot down, and so had better be burned on a bonfire; do not, however, leave the bonfire ashes for long after the fire is over, because a great deal of the goodness in them will have been made soluble during burning and will quickly wash away in the rain. So add them as soon as they are ready.

Half-woody material such as cabbage stalks may also be burned if you do not think it will rot down quickly enough. It is a pity to do so, though, because it will contribute much more to the value of your compost if it is all used instead of half its goodness being allowed to go up in smoke. So if you can spare the time and energy the best thing is to chop up the stalk into short lengths with a sharp spade, as shown. After chopping them, stamp on the pieces of stalk to soften them and then add them to the heap. The correct way to make a compost heap is in layers, as shown; a simple pile like this is quite enough to produce compost even if you do not want to be bothered with making a bin, but it is more difficult to keep in shape and because it cannot be kept so compact and tends to dry out, it will

take much longer to turn into usable compost. The first thing to do, whether using a bin or not, is to form a layer of the sort of vegetable waste we have just been examining. If it consists of soft and harder material mix them together as much as possible. Then tread this layer down and water it if it is dry. You may then sprinkle it with one of the compost activators which can be bought from garden stores; this is not strictly necessary, but it can speed things up a bit. Or a cheaper way of doing the same thing is to sprinkle the layer with ammonium sulphate. Then cover this with a thin layer of soil. On this put another layer of vegetable waste, sprinkle with activator, add another layer of earth and so on until you have completed the heap. The height of the heap will of course depend on the amount of material you have, but the higher you can make it, up to about the height of a man, the better.

The reason why, within limits, the bigger the heap the better the compost it makes is simply that big heaps get hotter than small ones, and the

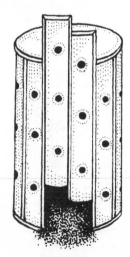

Circular bin

Chopping cabbage stalk

generation of a great deal of heat is a sign of good compost-making. When the heap is in full action it should reach such a temperature that if you thrust your hand into it you cannot bear to keep it there for more than a few seconds.

Other materials besides those already mentioned will make good compost: anything in fact that is organic vegetable matter, in other words anything that has been alive and would otherwise be wasted. Should you be able to get spent hops from a brewery, they make excellent compost; most of the taste will have gone in the brewing of beer, but there will still be plenty of goodness in them. Sawdust or wood shavings are also good materials, but there is one problem with them: in order to attack the hard, woody cells and break them down into something useful, the bacteria have to have a good supply of nitrogen. If they cannot obtain it from the wood, which is quite hard to digest, they will take it from the softer and more easily digested materials in the compost. As a result, you could find yourself with nitrogen-deficient compost, and when this is applied

to the soil it could in its turn take much-needed nitrogen from your vegetables and leave them starved. Fortunately there is quite an easy way to prevent this. When adding sawdust or wood shavings to your heap, sprinkle them liberally with ammonium sulphate. The bacteria actually prefer their nitrogen in that form and will therefore gobble it greedily up and leave the soil alone.

Some of the very best ingredients for making good compost are several of the common weeds, such as nettles, docks, pokeweed, annual sow-thistle, hemp nettle and pigweed—all juicy, leafy plants that break down very easily under bacterial action. If you know somebody who has a garden full of weeds of this kind, ask if you may cut them down and take them away. The weed-infested gardener will most likely thank you warmly, and you and your compost will be the beneficiaries.

There are certain weeds, though, that should be avoided at all costs. They are the ones with strong, perennial, creeping roots, such as bindweed, creeping buttercup, quackgrass, and Canada thistle. Even the heat of a well-made compost heap cannot be guaranteed to kill them; some seem to have discovered the secret of immortality, however hard you try to kill them, and if you introduce a piece of live root from them into your soil from your compost, you may give yourself a lifetime's trouble trying to get rid of them.

Basically there are two ways of using compost—either by digging it into the lower part of the top spit (in the subsoil it may be wasted) or applied to the surface of the soil. If you have enough compost, use it in both ways. If not keep it for using on the surface of the soil as a mulch. It will keep the soil moist beneath, stop the ground from cracking and smother weeds—or if some weeds grow in it they can be pulled out of it with very little effort.

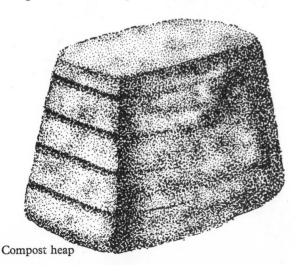
Compost heap

9. Preparing the surface

AFTER DIGGING your ground and leaving it lumpy for winter frosts to break it down, you will want to get a good surface (gardeners call it 'tilth') when seed-sowing time comes.

First make the earth roughly even and firm by treading it down across the plot from one side to the other, as shown. This should be done in early spring, when the soil is starting to dry. Do not treat more ground at a time than you need for immediate sowing; if you leave it for long it may settle into a hard surface which is almost as difficult to sow seed on as if it had never been dug at all.

The clods of earth should crumble quite easily if the ground is in the right state—that is, not too wet and not too dry. In those conditions raking is quite a simple operation, but there is one thing you must be careful of. After that first light firming with the feet, do not walk about more than necessary. In particular, *never tread on any part of the ground again once that part has been finished*. Begin at one corner of the plot and walk backwards, so that you do not have to retrace your steps.

If you are right-handed, the best way to use a rake is to hold the upper end of the handle with your right hand, palm downwards, and the lower part of the handle with your left hand, palm upwards. Do not stoop or crouch, but bend slightly forwards, with your arms fully extended so that the handle is as nearly horizontal as possible. This will make sure that the teeth of the rake go into the ground at the correct angle. Then by swinging your arms comfortably to and fro you will find that the rake sweeps backwards and forwards, crumbling the surface into a fine tilth with very little effort.

Big stones and other undesirables will be caught by the teeth and swept backwards, as shown, so that you can remove them. If the ground is very stony, have a bucket by you so that you can throw the stones into it as you go along, and so stop them from forming a heavy accumulation that has to be dragged backwards by sheer force.

Crush any lumps of earth as you come to them—they should crumble quite easily. When you have finished, the surface should be left fine and even, but at the same time soft and yielding, so that it will be easy to draw a nice, even seed drill in it.

But suppose, as is sometimes the case, that you have not been able to get your ground dug until the frosts are over. How can you manage to get a good surface for sowing? It may be necessary in that case to use a heavier tool than the rake—for example one of the sharp-toothed cultivators shown in the

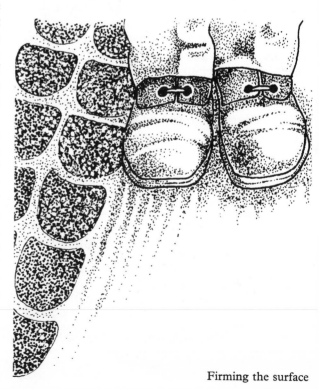

Firming the surface

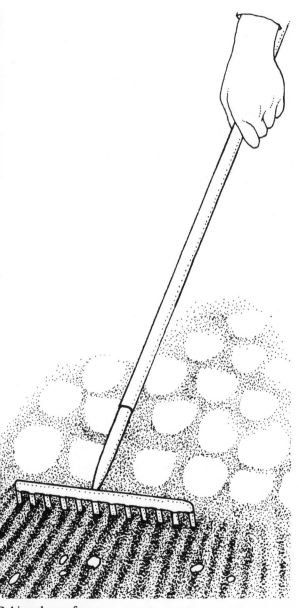

section *Labor-saving devices*. But if you use such an implement be careful to work with a *raking* movement. Do not try to beat the clods of earth to pieces; this would not only be extremely tiring but would compress the soil, so that the first rain would wash it into a solid mass. Finish off with the rake to get your final tilth.

Never be too thorough with your raking. It can be so easy that the novice lets it run away with him and tramps to and fro raking vigorously, until the surface is completely smooth and unblemished. Unfortunately, though, the ground has become so trodden down in the process that it might just as well not have been dug in the first place.

The reason why it is so important that the surface of the soil should not be too smooth is that the roots of plants need air and water. A smooth surface stops them from getting a proper supply of either. It can become so battered down by rain that it forms a hard crust, which neither air nor water can penetrate. The rain either runs off or stays on the surface till it evaporates, and the roots get no benefit from it at all. That is why in such circumstances plants can suffer from drought after heavy rain.

Also, not only is the surface too hard to let in enough air for the roots to breathe properly but it will not let out the gases they give off; as a result, the roots become suffocated and die. It is very important never to allow the soil to get into this condition of forming a hard crust. Always leave a certain amount of loose material on the surface—not only crumbs of soil but small stones. If your soil is so fine that it is difficult to prevent a hard crust from forming, get some sharp sand or grit and rake that into the surface. It will work wonders.

Raking the surface

10. Sowing and planting

WHEN you have got a good sowing surface or 'tilth' on your soil by the methods described in the section *Preparing the surface*, the time has come to sow the seed at last.

Sowing

Vegetable seeds are nearly always sown in drills. A drill is simply a shallow groove in the soil into which the seed is sprinkled and then covered over with earth again.

It is a very easy matter to make a drill. All you have to do is to stretch your garden line across the plot and draw the edge of the blade of your hoe along it as shown, so that the corner plows into the surface of the ground, piling the soil up neatly along the side of the drill.

Seed drills are usually made very shallow, unless the seeds are large: this means in most cases an inch deep or less. If they were made too deep the seed would probably fail to germinate, or if it did the seedlings would have difficulty in bursting through the weight of earth above them. The depth, however, varies with the nature of the crop and the size of seed. Exact instructions therefore on the depth of the drill required are given in this book

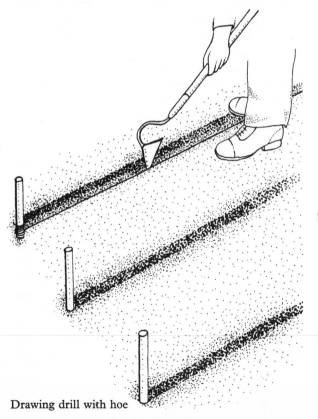

Drawing drill with hoe

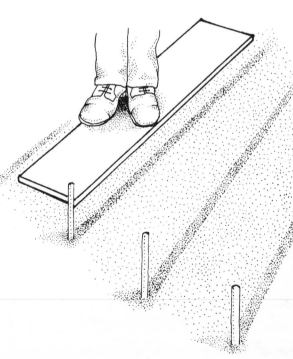

Standing between rows on boards

in the sections on each kind of vegetable. One point you have to watch is that the garden line is stretched really tight, otherwise it will sag in the middle and your drill will be curved instead of straight.

A possible cause of trouble is that a great many crops are sown in the spring, while the ground is still quite moist, so that treading about on the soil between rows during sowing may spoil the surface by trampling it down. An easy way to avoid this problem is to place a board on the ground beside the row, as shown, and walk on that; it will distribute your weight and prevent foot prints.

When the drill has been drawn the seed is sown thinly along the bottom. Do not sprinkle it thickly; that not only wastes seed but makes the later operation of thinning much harder and more tedious. It also overcrowds the seedlings and so gives them a bad start. The quantity of seed required is given in this book for each vegetable. *Do not exceed it.*

Never, as some gardeners do, tear the corner off the seed packet and shake the seed straight from it into the drill. If you do, you will get mounds of seed in some places and none at all in others. Besides, it is very wasteful because it uses much more seed. The best way to sow is by hand as pictured here. First, pour a quantity of seed into the palm of your left hand, then take a pinch of seed between the thumb and first two fingers of your right hand, and, holding it just above the ground to prevent it from being blown away, let it trickle out between your fingers into the drill as you move along the row.

When that pinch of seed has been used up, take another, and so on until the row has been finished. Sow *thinly*; with practice you will soon learn to control the trickle so as to give the right flow of seed.

To cover the seed after sowing, many people

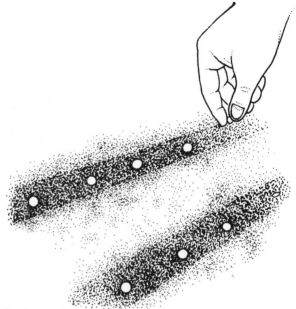

Sowing seeds

simply rake back into the drill the ridge of soil that was heaped along the side by the hoe. That is not the best way to do things, because it leaves the soil so loose that the moisture which the seed needs for germination and growth is in danger of drying out.

A better way is to close the drill by foot (see p. 36). Placing one foot on each side of the drill, shuffle along from one end to the other, pushing the soil in so that it covers the seed. Do not be afraid to use your feet quite hard, so that the surface is made firm.

After shuffling along the row in this way, you will probably want to tidy things up with a rake. Do this in the way shown. Walk backwards along the row, raking lightly as you go, so as to leave an even surface. Rake to and fro along the row, not sideways, or you will shift some of the seeds and find plants growing beside the row instead of in it.

Planting

Most vegetables are sown in the place where they are to spend the whole of their lives until they are harvested. With some kinds, however, that would be very wasteful of ground, because they take so long to grow full-size that if they were shown in their final quarters they would be wasting space that could be used for quicker growing things. In this case, sowings are made in a seed bed and later on when the seedlings are big enough they are transplanted to the place where they will remain until they are used. Nearly all the members of the cabbage family are treated in this way.

Transplanting is bound to be something of a shock to the seedlings, since it is a surgical operation. However carefully you go about it, you cannot help damaging some of the roots. Try therefore to make the damage as little as possible, by digging up the plant carefully (a small hand fork or trowel is best for this) with as much soil as possible on the roots,

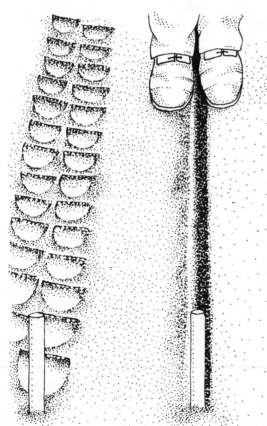

Treading

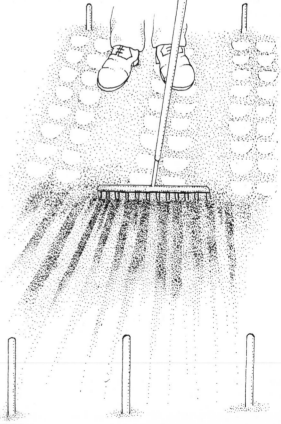

Raking

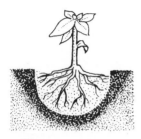

Transplanting seedlings

and plant it in its new home as quickly as you can, so that it does not dry out. Remember that roots which have been allowed to become dry and shrivelled are even less likely to be able to grow properly again than ones that have been torn in digging them up; wounds will often heal, but tissue that has died will remain dead. Transplanting is best done during showery weather. Then the seedling will come out of the ground more easily, will not be in so much danger of drying, and will settle down quicker in its new home. The planting hole can be made with a blunt-pointed piece of wood, but it is better if dug out with a trowel or hand fork. Then the roots can be spread out properly, as shown, instead of being all bunched together, which is not good for their growth.

Do not bury the plant too deeply. The correct depth for transplanting is so that the seed leaves (the two lowest leaves) show above the surface of the ground. Holding the plant at this depth, fill the earth carefully into the hole; make sure that it completely surrounds the roots, leaving no air pockets. Finish off by pressing the earth *firmly* round the base of the plant. Treading round it with the heel of your boot is a good way to make sure it is firm enough. To check this, take a leaf between your thumb and forefinger and pull upwards. If the leaf tears off but the plant remains in the ground, it is firm enough.

Lastly, water the plant well in to settle the soil around its roots.

Thinning

When your seedling plants start to emerge from the ground, they need thinning. This is a boring, tedious job. The beginner may wonder why it is necessary at all. Why not simply sow one seed in each place where you want a vegetable, and leave it at that? The answer is that not all seeds, even the most expensive ones, will germinate. Besides, if you remove the weakest seedlings, you have only the best and strongest ones left. If you sow thinly in the first place, less thinning will be needed, but some will still have to be done. Take a container with you so that the thinnings can be dropped into it as you go along and then put on the compost heap instead of being left around. You will find the final distance apart, after thinning, given for each vegetable in this book.

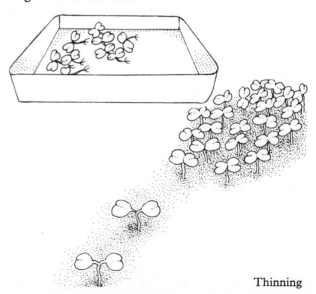

Thinning

37

11. Manures and fertilizers

To THE dedicated vegetable gardener, there is no more attractive sight in the world than a horse in a stable yard picking its way through rich, steaming manure full of golden straw. Nothing can be better for the soil, both as plant food and as a fine improver of soil structure, than good old-fashioned manure, provided it is in the right condition—that is to say, well rotted and neither wet and sticky (in which case it will do the soil more harm than good) nor bone-dry (in which case it will be very difficult to wet it again.)

Since horses on farms have largely been replaced by tractors and other machines, which instead of enriching the soil only pollute the air, there is very little stable manure about, so if you manage to obtain some of this precious material make sure you use it to the best advantage. Unless it has become well decomposed, it would probably be best added to the compost heap in layers, instead of chemical activator (see the section *Making and using compost*).

Manure dug into the ground in a fresh state will not only lose a great deal of its plant food value, which may well disappear in clouds of gas, but may make the soil sour and soggy. Even the most robustly growing vegetables can only take up a certain amount of food, so do not over-feed your soil or much of the goodness will be wasted. As we have already seen, in the section *Improving the soil*, most ground that has not grown vegetables before will contain enough plant food to last for a year or two. But you will want to know what to use in order to replace the essential plant foods that vegetables take away from the soil when you remove them.

The three elements of plant food that most commonly need replacing are, as we have also seen, nitrogen, phosphorus and potassium.

Nitrogen is vital to the whole plant, but particularly to the green parts about the ground, both leaf and stem. It is therefore specially important to all green vegetables, lettuces and others like them, and to rhubarb, celery, asparagus and such-like.

Phosphorus is also needed by all the plant. It is of crucial importance to photosynthesis (the process by which plants use the sun's energy for growth) and helps to form flowers and fruit, including peas and beans. It keeps vegetables firm, and so balances nitrogen, which in excess makes them flabby, and encourages rooting, especially in the early stages of a seedling's life.

Potassium is also found throughout the plant, and is essential to healthy growth. It is needed particularly by the underground parts and is therefore specially important to potatoes and to all root crops such as carrots, beets and parsnips. It also balances nitrogen.

As you can see, different types of vegetable use up different proportions of the various plant foods. That is a very important reason for planning the rotation of crops.

Organic manures

ANIMAL MANURES These not only contain all three of the important plant foods just described (and trace elements in the necessary tiny amounts as well) but also have the great advantage over artificial fertilizers of forming humus. Inorganic chemical fertilizers supply only food in the form of salts, but animal manures turn into fertile soil as well. The three animal manures most commonly used—though becoming scarce now—are horse, cow and pig manure. Of these, horse manure is generally the most balanced, with a good proportion of phosphorus and potassium. Pig manure is usually richest in nitrogen.

The bedding material used in the manure is as important as the dung itself. The best is straw or

Manure ready for use

peat moss. Nowadays such things as sawdust or wood shavings are sometimes used, and they take a good deal longer to rot down.

All animal manures generate heat when stacked, but horse manure tends to be warm and dry by nature, while both cow and pig manure tend to be cold and wet. Therefore stable manure is specially suitable on heavy soils, which need warmth and drainage, and the other two on light soils, which they bind together, so helping them to retain moisture.

POULTRY MANURE You may hear it said that the droppings of domestic fowls are three or four times as 'strong' as farmyard manure. That is not usually true. Weight for weight they tend to contain less phosphorus and potassium, though they may have as much nitrogen or even more.

The truth about poultry manure is not that it is 'stronger', but that it acts very quickly. That makes it a valuable stimulant to plants during growth. If used fresh, however, it might act so quickly as to burn the roots. A very good way to deal with the droppings is to spread them out to dry somewhat and then mix them with at least twice their own bulk of crumbly earth or sand. This preparation can be lightly forked or hoed into the soil between rows of plants. Do not use it in the fall between green crops that are intended to stand the winter; its high nitrogen content could cause them to make soft growth which might be damaged by frost.

HOP MANURE Prepared hop manure is quite expensive to buy, but if there is a nearby brewery that will let you have their spent hops, dig them in or add them to your compost heap.

WOOD ASHES are the cheapest source of potash, but this is in a highly soluble form and so the goodness is quickly washed away by rain. Either keep them under cover or include them in the compost heap, which will absorb most of the potash instead of letting it go to waste.

BONE MEAL is a valuable slow-acting plant food containing many elements and a rich source of phosphorus.

HOOF AND HORN MEAL is also slow to break down and releases its goodness, in particular nitrogen, over a long period. Like bone meal, it is best sprinkled on the surface and lightly hoed or raked in to give an extra boost during the growing season.

SEAWEED extract is used in the manufacture of some excellent liquid feeds which can be bought at garden stores. Such feeds are usually diluted with water and can either be sprayed on the foliage or watered on the soil to keep up the strength and productivity of such heavily cropped plants as tomatoes and cucumbers.

Lime

As soon as you start growing vegetables, some friend is almost certain to say 'Give the ground plenty of lime'. There seems to be a belief among many gardeners that lime has magic properties. This belief must be responsible for an enormous amount of unnecessary lime being wasted on gardens every year. It is quite easy to tell whether your ground needs lime or not. An inexpensive testing kit can be bought at most garden stores, which, if you follow the easy instructions, will soon show the pH of your soil. The term pH simply means how acid or alkali your soil is. The figure 7 means it is neutral; below 7 it is acid and above 7 it is alkaline (limy).

Adding lime unnecessarily is not only wasteful but bad. *Lime is not used primarily as a plant food.* (True, it contains calcium, but plants are hardly ever deficient in that.) It makes certain plant foods more soluble and others less soluble, so if it is not used correctly it can make matters a good deal worse for your soil and your plants. Most vegetables prefer a neutral or very slightly acid soil, so only if the pH of your ground is well below 7 will you need to add lime. The best form is hydrate of lime or ground limestone, which can be sprinkled over the ground, preferably in the spring, just enough to whiten the surface, and then raked in. Never let lime come in contact with fresh farmyard manure, or nitrogen will be lost into the air as ammonia gas. More information is given in the section *Rotation of crops* about when and where to apply lime. Properly used, it will sweeten the soil and improve its structure, so that it becomes easier to work.

Artificial fertilizers

These are chemical substances which can give quick results if sprinkled on the soil during the growing season. There are nitrogen-yielding ones, such as ammonium sulphate; phosphorus-yielding ones, such as *superphosphate*; and potassium-yielding ones, such as potassium sulphate. Since these are all strong chemicals which can easily do damage if used by themselves, it is much better for the amateur to buy a complete fertilizer containing all three elements. This can be applied in spring, just before sowing, or as a top dressing between growing crops—but be careful not to get it on the plants themselves or it might scorch them.

Green manuring

This is an easy and cheap way of adding humus and nourishment to the soil. When a patch of ground is going to be left bare for several weeks during the growing season, sow it fairly thickly with a quick-growing green crop, such as ryegrass, buckwheat or vetches; these last are specially good because, like all leguminous crops, they extract nitrogen from the air. When the plants have grown a few inches high, and before they have time to form flowers and seeds, dig them in, making sure they are completely buried, and they will rot down to enrich the soil.

Another very good reason for green manuring is that the latest research has shown that plant foods in bare ground can very quickly disappear from the topsoil and drain into the subsoil, where they are wasted. The plants used in green manuring prevent this from happening by taking up the foods into their roots, stems and leaves instead of allowing them to be drained away. When the plants rot down in the soil, they release those foods in a form that only becomes slowly soluble as it is worked on by soil bacteria, so it provides nourishment for your vegetable crops over a long period of time. In addition, green manure differs from all other kinds of manure by actually producing energy from sunlight as it grows, and that energy is added to the soil for the benefit of future crops.

12. Rotation of crops

INDIVIDUAL vegetables are dealt with in separate chapters later in the book. In planning out the use of your plot, however, this simple diagram will show you how to manage it throughout the seasons according to the treatment of the soil that different kinds of vegetable need. For the purposes of this handy guide only those crops that are going to occupy the ground for some time are shown. Salad crops—lettuces and radishes—are sown in succession, a little at a time, throughout the season on any suitable piece of ground between rows of other things that have not yet filled up all the space. By the time these grow to full size, the lettuces and radishes will have been gathered and eaten, since they are quick-growing catch-crops.

ROTATION Correct rotation of crops is a very important feature of a well-managed plot. If the same kind of vegetable is grown in the same spot year after year it will deplete the ground, since each kind has its special requirements, and it will almost certainly become prey to a build-up of pests and diseases. Particularly prone to this are potatoes, which if grown in the same place will build up such an eel worm population in the soil that they will cease to give a worthwhile crop at all. The best rotation for the amateur is a three-year rotation: the plot is divided into three, and each in turn gets a treatment in year 1 of manuring, in year 2 of liming and in year 3 of being used for crops that do better without either.

MANURE PLOT The best manure to put the soil into good heart is good, rich, bulky organic stuff such as horse, cow or pig manure containing plenty of straw; but it must be well rotted or it may be too strong for the plant roots. Unfortunately, in our increasingly urbanized society such stuff is becoming scarce and expensive. Alternatives are well made compost as described in an earlier chapter, peat, spent hops or similar organic waste material. It should be dug well into the soil, but not buried too deeply or its goodness will be lost.

The easiest way is to spread the manure over the surface of the ground before digging. Then it will be automatically put into the soil as digging proceeds, and will finally be incorporated when the surface is raked.

LIME PLOT Most vegetables grow best in ground with a certain amount of lime. Lime sweetens the soil if it is becoming too acid, helps to break it up and make it more crumbly, and so helps to make a good, fine seed bed, and wards off—or at least reduces the risk of—certain diseases, such as the horrible slime fungus, called clubroot, which attacks members of the cabbage family. Lime should never be applied at the same time as, or allowed to come in contact with, animal manure: if it does there will be a nasty smell of ammonia and most of the value of the manure will be lost.

Not all soil needs, or will benefit from, lime applications every three years: a cheap and handy soil testing kit will tell you whether yours needs it or not.

ROOT CROPS The third year of the rotation, a third of the plot is left without either manure or lime. This is particularly useful for root crops, since if carrots or parsnips come in contact with anything like fresh manure in the soil, they tend to grow forked and branched rootlets instead of sending down good straight roots in search of nourishment and water in the lower layers of the soil. Also in this part of the plot peas and beans thrive; like all the leguminous vegetables, they have their own way of producing their own nitrogenous fertilizer (the most important of all) from the air by means of nitrogen-fixing bacteria in the roots. No further enrichment should be needed until this ground is due for its manuring next year, though a sprinkling of artificial fertilizer may be given.

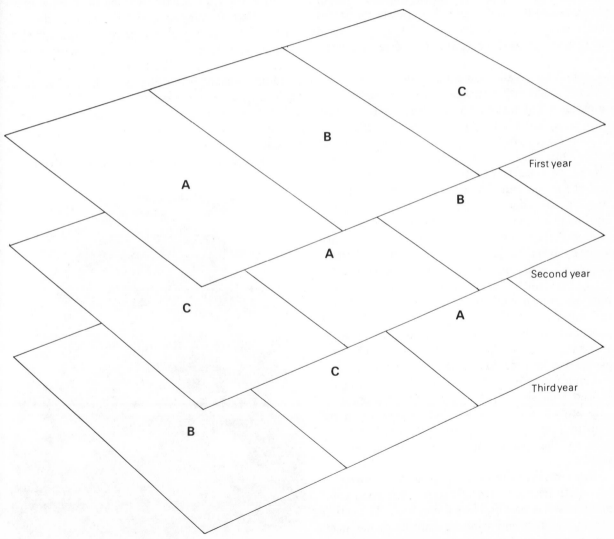

A-manure plot; B-lime plot; C-root crop

13. No-digging methods

THIS QUITE NEW development in vegetable-growing means quite different things to different people. To some it means a highly artificial modern technique made possible by the development of such types of plastic material as polythene. The illustration shows one example of this kind of no-digging method being used to produce early, effort-free and clean potatoes. The tubers are sprouted (as shown in the section *Potatoes*) and planted in shallow holes in the ground, made with a trowel, so that the sprouts are uppermost and just below soil level. When a row of potatoes has been planted, 1 foot (30 cm.) apart, in this way, sprinkle slug bait among them and cover with black plastic. Anchor one end of the plastic, with earth and a few heavy stones, at the end of the row and then unwind it over the tubers, burying the edges in the soil as you go along, and weigh it down with heavy stones along the edges to stop it from being lifted by wind. With a sharp knife or razor blade make a slit in the polythene above each sprout and gently coax the sprout through it. By midsummer there should be a crop of early potatoes, which you can gather by carefully lifting the edges of the plastic. Replace it over the small tubers left to allow them to complete their growth.

That is one of the many ways in which black plastic can be used in the vegetable garden. More and more people are finding that by covering the ground with sheeting between rows of crops they help growth during dry weather by keeping in the moisture, and they have very little weeding to do because the plastic suppresses the growth of weeds.

Research over the past few years has shown that bare earth between rows of vegetables is not a good thing, however neat and tidy it may look. The action of sun and rain and wind on bare earth has been shown to damage the structure of the soil, causing it to crack and lose not only moisture but plant foods and destroying a large proportion of the useful soil bacteria. After all, bare soil is not a natural thing, so when users of plastic sheeting on their gardens are accused of doing something unnatural they are quite entitled to say that it is not as unnatural as digging and hoeing. It is true that nature most certainly does not dig manures and other humus-forming substances into the ground. Animals leave their droppings on the surface, wild plants grow and die and decay on the surface and leaves drop in the fall and form a layer on the surface. True, they do not stay entirely on the surface but are pulled down below by earthworms and other soil inhabi-

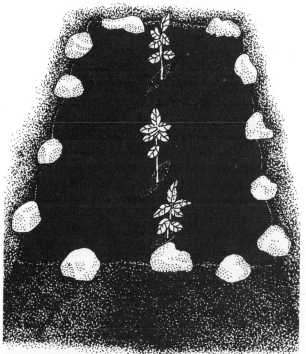

Black plastic mulch

44

Sprouted potatoes

tants that exist to recycle dead and decaying matter. Even so, the humus-forming material that in natural conditions enriches the earth each year stays in the top few inches of soil.

Those who believe in no-digging methods, because such methods are in accordance with the way nature does things, argue therefore that nothing should be put *into* the soil but only on *top* of it. Many of them refuse to use any chemical fertilizers because they say that such inorganic mineral salts are not formed naturally except deep down in the subsoil and underlying rocks, from which they are extracted by the deepest roots of the tallest trees, which then return these minerals to the top soil in the form of fallen leaves.

Believers in natural ways do not accept plastic because it is a man-made synthetic product. The mulches (which means surface dressings) that they put on the soil consist not of plastic therefore but of compost or well matured leaf mold. Seeds are sown on this layer and then covered with more. During the growing season, more of the same material (or, if there is not enough of it, damp peat or even sawdust) is added as a mulch on each side of the row to keep in moisture and keep down weeds; if any weeds do appear they are much more easily pulled out of the mulch than out of the hard earth.

Some people who have changed to no-digging methods say they will never go back to the old spade-fork-and-hoe routine again. Experiment, in a small way at first, on part of your vegetable patch. If you get good results, the no-digging technique might save you a lot of work.

Many supporters of no-digging methods are opposed to artificial fertilizers, because the word artificial suggests unnatural, or even decadent. Such people will, of course, object to the adding of any chemical to the mulching material. That is perfectly reasonable if the mulch consists of soft, well-rotted things such as mature compost or decayed leaves, which have been thoroughly digested by bacteria. If however the mulch is made up of undigested woody material such as sawdust, there is a danger that the bacteria, which need a constant supply of nitrogen, will take it from the soil—since there is very little available nitrogen in sawdust—and so starve the plants. A little high-nitrogen chemical fertilizer mixed with the sawdust will solve the problem, since bacteria rather like their nitrogen in artificial form.

14. Garden friends

As soon as it is known that you are going to grow your own vegetables, friends and relations and neighbors will eagerly tell you horror stories about all the pests and diseases that are lying in wait to ruin your efforts. Advertisements put out by manufacturers of garden chemicals will inform you that unless you spray and dust all the time with their products, your crops will finish up by being eaten by the nastier forms of wild life instead of by you.

No wonder the gardening novice often becomes convinced that every living creature he meets on his vegetable patch is his natural enemy, and so tries to kill everything indiscriminately. Yet if people only knew it, their plants have quite as many friends as enemies. It stands to reason that this must be so; if plants had no friends but only enemies they would have died out long ago, so let us have a look at some of our friends to keep our spirits up.

BIRDS   Never kill birds. Most of the time they do very little harm and a great deal of good.

The robin, for instance, eats large quantities of insects, grubs and other pests during the course of the season, as do all its relations in the thrush family. The thrush itself is also a most efficient killer of snails, which it hits on a hard stone to crack open the shell and get at its favorite meat inside. True, many birds peck up newly sown ground, but it is quite simple to protect against them by stretching black thread along the rows and so force the birds to give up their work of destruction and turn to the useful job of eating weed seeds instead.

If it were not for birds there would be a massive increase in the number of pests, and the growing of vegetables would become much harder.

BATS   They help to reduce the insect population, even though most people tend to hate them.

Among their favorite foods are beetles, particularly leaf chafers, May beetles and click beetles. Rest assured that their blood sucking relatives only reside in the tropics.

SHREWS   Unlike mice, which can do a great deal of damage by eating seeds and plants, shrews are almost entirely carnivorous. They have an enormous appetite for such small creatures and can eat in a day their own weight in insects, worms, snails, slugs and beetles.

FROGS AND TOADS   These also eat large numbers of pests, including slugs, caterpillars, grubs, and other plant-destroying pests, which they catch with their long tongues.

CENTIPEDES   Millions of centipedes must be killed during the course of the year by gardeners who think they are pests. In fact they are extremely valuable. They feed on all kinds of pests in the soil, which they kill with their powerful poisoned claws. The trouble is that centipedes are often mistaken for the harmful millepedes which do a great deal of damage by gnawing their way through roots and tubers. Yet there is no need to confuse the two creatures. Centipedes have fewer legs and can move much more quickly than millepedes. So if you come across a brown, shiny creature like the one shown

Centipede

Robin

here scuttling hurriedly through the soil, it is a centipede and should be left to go on its way in peace.

In fact there is a general rule about insects and other creepy-crawlies that you find in the ground. *If it moves quickly leave it alone.* The reason is quite simple. Since plants do not move about, the vegetarian pests that attack them can do so at their leisure, and so do not have to be quick in their movements. On the other hand, the carnivores, pest eating creatures which are our friends, are hunters, and like all hunters they have to look sharp about it if their prey is not to escape.

LADYBUGS   There are many different species of ladybug, the commonest being the ones with bright red wing cases marked with black spots. The larvae (young) of ladybugs, shown here beside an adult, are commonly called 'crocodiles' because of their appearance. They feed greedily upon those most widespread of all vegetable pests the aphids (green-fly, blackfly and their unpleasant relatives).

LACEWING FLIES   These also live on aphids, or rather their larvae do. The commonest lacewing fly has pale green, almost transparent wings delicately traced with veins. When attacked it gives out a disgusting smell. The larva, shown here beside an adult, is a strange looking creature covered with bristles and with a hearty appetite for aphids.

PRAYING MANTIS   Related to the grasshopper and devourers of a whole range of insects, capturing them with their powerful front legs. The baby mantises begin eating aphids from the day they are born. Like ladybugs they are available via mail order—see the ads in gardening magazines.

HOVERFLIES   There are several species, but they all have the same trick of hovering motionless in the air, their wings going so fast that you can hardly see them move, and making sudden little darts and then remaining motionless again. Most species are striped rather like wasps and they all have young like the one shown here—rather flat, semitranslucent

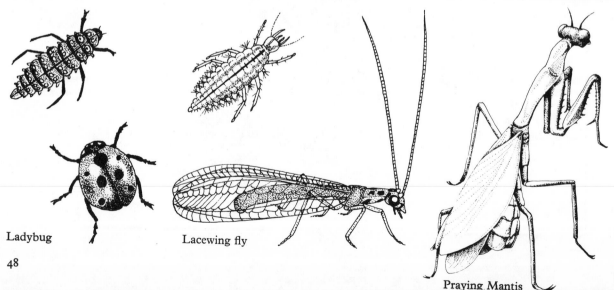

Ladybug

Lacewing fly

Praying Mantis

48

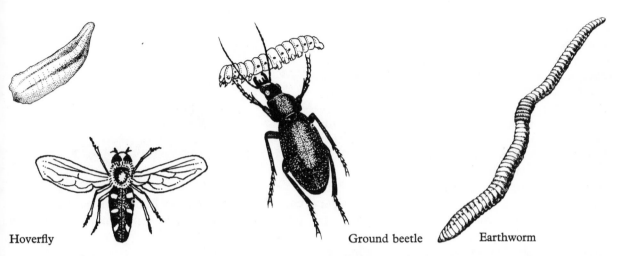

Hoverfly   Ground beetle   Earthworm

and looking rather like a slim miniature slug. Their way of consuming aphids is highly efficient, and fascinating, though rather horrible to watch. They seize the aphid, lift it up, puncture it, suck out the whole of its insides, and then spit out the empty skin. One hoverfly larva, moving steadily along an infested plant, can disembowel hundreds of aphids an hour.

ICHNEUMONS There are very many different kinds of these strange parasitic creatures. A typical species, which is particularly valuable to vegetable growers, is very small and has a slim-waisted black body. It lays its eggs right in the body of that great nuisance the caterpillar of the cabbage white butterfly. In a few days, the eggs hatch out into tiny maggots, which eat away the caterpillar's flesh, so that it dies a lingering death. If you find the maggot-eaten corpse of a caterpillar, do not destroy it but leave it for the flies to emerge and continue their good work of destroying caterpillars.

GROUND BEETLES There are many of these soil

inhabitants which feed chiefly on insects. They are usually black, brown, blue or green and rather metallic in appearance. The kind shown here is the violet ground beetle; it is seen just starting to attack a soil caterpillar or cutworm, a pest which kills plants by biting them off at soil level but which this time cannot escape being killed in its turn by the beetle's murderous claws.

EARTHWORMS Darwin pointed out in 1882 that earthworms were one of the gardener's best friends. They both plow and fertilize the soil, so improving both its texture and nutritional content, as well as naturally aerating it. They perform invaluable work in the compost pile too. The earthworm population in your soil can be boosted by the addition of farm-raised specimens (often advertized in the garden magazines) or by rearing your own.

15. Garden foes

UNFORTUNATELY, there are large numbers of pests whose natural food consists of the vegetables you are trying to grow. Those which attack particular crops are dealt with in this book under the heading of the individual vegetable concerned, and so are diseases and their remedies.

A few pests, however, show little preference for one kind of plant but attack almost anything that they can find. We will deal with some of those universal pests in this section. The majority are insects (there are after all over a million different species of insect in the world) but let us consider some of the larger pests first.

MICE   These do their worst damage by eating—or more irritatingly gnawing pieces out of—vegetables stored for the winter. They are extremely clever at getting into buildings and have been known to carry off the whole of a stored crop in one night to hide it in their nest. At the beginning of the growing season they can be a serious nuisance, burrowing in the soil and eating newly-sown seeds, especially large ones such as peas and beans. Traps can be a help, but put them where pets cannot get caught by them (a dome of wire netting over them is quite good for this). Poison bait can be bought also; it is put in little heaps where the mice can get at it but domestic animals cannot, and has to be renewed daily until no more is taken, because it usually takes several doses to kill a mouse.

RABBITS   If there are many of these about they can completely wreck your attempts at vegetable growing. Snares are sometimes used, but besides being horrible they can cause suffering and death to cats and other friendly creatures. Probably the only efficient protection against rabbits is to surround the whole vegetable patch with a wirenetting fence, high

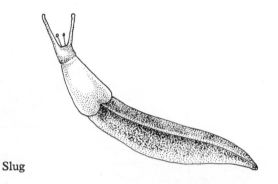

Slug

enough to prevent them from jumping it and sunk far enough into the soil to stop them from burrowing under it.

SLUGS   There are many different species. Between them they do an enormous amount of damage, particularly the slim gray kind shown here, which gnaws plants both above and below ground. As will be seen in the section *Natural pest control*, slugs are not by nature wholly destructive but scavengers of decaying parts of plants; gardeners, being tidy, leave them only live plants to eat instead. However, that is no comfort if your precious seedlings are being attacked. You can buy liquid slug-killer which, diluted with water, is sprayed over the rows of young vegetables, or there are slug baits which you scatter among the plants; slugs eat the baits with great relish, and die. Go round next morning and pick up the corpses; one or two may not be quite dead and can be destroyed before they have time to recover.

SNAILS   These also include a large number of different species. The ordinary garden snail shown here is the commonest. Although there are not so many of them in most places as there are slugs, and therefore they cause less widespread destruction,

Mice

individually they can do more damage simply because they eat more. They can be killed by the same methods as slugs.

WIREWORMS The yellowish-brown, hard-skinned grub shown here, and commonly known as the wireworm, is perhaps the most widespread and destructive of all soil pests. It feeds greedily on plant roots and tubers for four or five years before it turns into the adult click-beetle pictured beside it. Wireworms are most numerous and destructive on newly dug grass-land. They are not easy to control, but there are modern chemical powders that will kill many and keep the others at bay if you apply them to the top layers of soil before sowing or planting.

WOODCHUCKS (or GROUNDHOGS) These mammals are a major pest throughout most of the country with the exception of the extreme south. They weigh as much as 10 pounds and have short legs and tail, and a broad body and head. Their appetite is enormous— they can devour as much as a pound of vegetables

per day. They can be effectively disposed of by fumigating the tunnels where they live with a special cartridge or carbon disulphide.

WHITEFLIES These troublesome creatures look, as shown here, rather like small moths, but they are no relations. They are in fact related to the aphids, or plant lice, and to the scale insects, and they have the nastiest habits of both. They breed so rapidly that they can become an alarming infestation within a week or two. From the masses of tiny eggs, laid on leaves to which each is attached by a hair-like stalk, larvae hatch out in vast quantities. They suck the sap and in this way weaken the plant; they then make matters worse by excreting a sticky substance known as honeydew which not only clogs the pores of the leaves, but soon grows a covering of a particularly unattractive fungus called sooty mold, which blackens everything. Whiteflies have been on the increase for several years, because many modern insecticides cannot penetrate their protective layer of wax. However, there are now some new sprays that do seem to kill them quite effectively so long

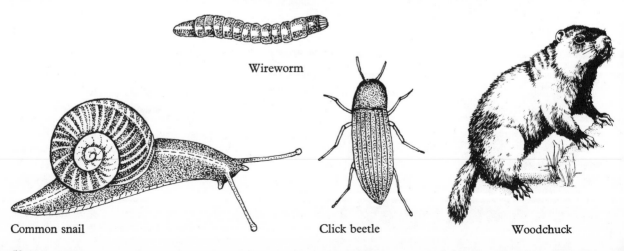

Wireworm

Common snail

Click beetle

Woodchuck

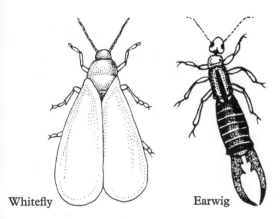

Whitefly   Earwig

Leafhopper

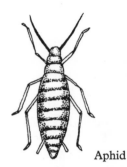

Aphid

as they are used early enough.

EARWIGS Of all the many species of this pest, the European earwig shown here is probably the one you know best, with its nasty-looking pair of pincers at its rear end. It is mainly a pest of flowers, such as dahlias and chrysanthemums, which it attacks mostly at night, damaging and distorting the blooms by gnawing them; but it can do considerable harm in the vegetable garden as well, where it particularly enjoys spoiling the heads of cauliflower and broccoli —which are of course flower buds. Fortunately a large number of modern insecticides—both dusts and sprays—are effective against earwigs if they are applied not only to the plants but to the soil round them, where these pests often hide.

LEAFHOPPERS These are also called frog hoppers, because of the frog-like leaps they make when disturbed. The naked green young suck the sap from leaves and shoots, and cover themselves with froth, as pictured here. They are not one of the worst of pests, but their sap-sucking can weaken such plants as peas and beans. Their foamy covering does not protect them from modern insecticide

sprays; in fact it makes sure that the spray wets them and so kills them.

APHIDS We have left these, the most widespread of all plant pests, till last. Known also as plant lice, the aphids form an enormous family—greenfly, blackfly, grey, yellow, red and brown. Not only do they seriously weaken plants by sucking the sap from them, but as they puncture them they can infect them with all kinds of diseases, just as mosquitoes can infect human beings with malaria. Because aphids are so widespread, there are more sprays sold against them than against any other pests. Highly effective they are too; aphids have no defences and are easily killed. However, you must keep a watch for them and be prepared to spray again at any time, because one pregnant female is so prolific that she can infest a plant with her young in a few days.

WARNING Not all insecticides are right for killing all pests, so make sure you buy the right one for the job. Also not all chemicals are suitable for all plants; some can be damaged, or even killed, by the wrong spray. Read what it says on the container before using any pesticide and *follow the instructions exactly*.

16. Natural pest control

SOME EXPERIENCED vegetable gardeners grow annual flowers of the marigold type, called *Tagetes*, alongside crops that are susceptible to certain kinds of pest. As you can see from the picture, the flowers are very attractive, but that is not why they are grown. It is believed by many people that the blossoms release a substance into the air that drives away such pests as whitefly; there is also a belief that secretions from their roots kill certain soil pests, particularly the destructive eelworm.

This is one of the many forms of natural pest-control that are being tried by gardeners who are worried about the effects of all the poisons that are sprayed on crops these days.

So many pests and diseases attack vegetables that it is impossible to list them all. A few, which attack many different crops, were described in the section *Garden foes*. Most, however, only attack certain plants, and the most troublesome of these are dealt with in the sections on particular vegetables, together with the most effective methods of control at the present time.

Things change, however. Chemicals that were thought safe turn out to be dangerous and are restricted or banned by law. New strains of pests appear which are immune to the products that used to kill them. So research laboratories turn out newer products still in an attempt to kill the superpests; and so it goes on, like the arms race, each new weapon of defense being overcome by a new method of attack, and all the time the cost of this chemical warfare gets higher. If the amateur gardener used all the new products as often as the manufacturers recommend, the price of growing your own vegetables would be more than you pay in the stores.

Besides, the corpses of the pests killed by modern chemicals remain poisonous and in their turn kill the birds and other innocent creatures that eat them.

That is why many people are turning to prevention rather than poisons.

The trap shown here cannot possibly harm anybody or anything but the pests it was designed to catch. It is simply a hollowed-out piece of potato with entrance tunnels cut into it and a stick in the top. Bury several of these under the surface of the soil at night; next morning take them up and destroy the soil pests—slugs, wireworms, millipedes and such things—which have crawled inside to feed.

There are hundreds of products on the market to kill aphids, the most widespread of all plant pest. Probably the most efficient are the organo-chlorine and the organo-phosphorus chemicals, but they are also the most dangerous, not only to wildlife and to human beings, but even to plants; in fact they must not be used on some crops at all. Because of the dangers, many people choose products based on natural insecticides from plants, such as rotenone or pyrethrum. Perhaps they are not quite such efficient killers, but they quickly break down into harmless substances (unlike the modern compounds, which

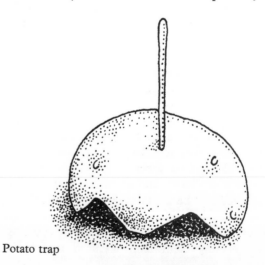

Potato trap

54

remain poisonous for years). Some people make up their own aphid-killing spray by boiling rhubarb leaves in water for half an hour and mixing the liquid with soap. Another good old fashioned spray against aphids and young caterpillars is made by boiling quassia chips (sold by pharmacists for killing lice in children's hair) in water.

Instead of using poison dusts in the soil to control the destructive cabbage maggot, some people are going back to preventing attacks by the device shown here, which is just a square of tarred roofing-paper with a hole cut in the middle and a slit from there to the side. One of these put round the base of each cabbage or related vegetable at planting time will make it difficult for the fly to lay her eggs near the plant; besides, she will be put off by the smell.

Other ways of repelling pests by confusing their sense of smell have been used by gardeners for a long time. For example, many people always grow onions between rows of carrots, because the carrot-fly is said to hate the smell of onions and the onion-fly to detest the smell of carrots.

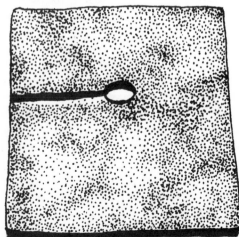

Roofing square

Tagetes

17. Potatoes

EVEN THE SMALLEST vegetable patch should grow some potatoes. Perhaps no other vegetable is quite so much improved by being home-grown: the care that can be given to planting, tending and particularly to digging up each tuber lovingly and gently makes the results so much better to eat than the commercially produced potato, which to show a profit has to be mechanically planted, mechanically cultivated and mechanically harvested, often getting so knocked about in the process that it has to be treated with bleaching chemicals to hide the bruises. So do try to grow some, even if it is only a row or two of 'new' or early varieties.

Soil and manuring

Potatoes should be grown in an open position with full light. Avoid, if you possibly can, any shade from trees or buildings, which not only makes the tops grow tall and weak and causes the crop to be poor, but encourages disease by preventing the leaves from drying out quickly after getting wet. Fungus diseases flourish on damp foliage. The soil should be deep and rich: if it has been double-dug, so much the better. Plenty of manure or compost will greatly benefit the crop, but it must be well rotted before the potatoes are planted. Tubers placed in contact with fresh manure are likely to develop all kinds of trouble. If the potatoes are being planted on newly broken-up grassland (particularly if the turf was chopped up and dug in) there will probably be enough goodness in the soil to grow a satisfactory crop of potatoes without needing any manure. In newly cultivated ground, potatoes make a most excellent first crop; they clean the ground, because their vigorous growth leaves the weeds far behind.

Sprouting

As soon as you get your seed potatoes, you should put them in a tray to sprout. A simple wooden affair such as the one shown in the drawing is ideal. Note the short wooden post at each corner; this is so that one tray can be stacked on another without damaging the tubers or keeping them in the dark. As you can see, the left-hand tuber in the drawing was allowed

Amount of 'seed' required
1 lb. (450 gr.) to every 5 ft. (c. 1.50 m.) of row.

When to plant
Early kinds in mid spring. Main crop in late spring.

Depth of drill
5 in. (c. 12 cm.).

Distance apart of rows
Early, 2 ft. (c. 60 cm.) Main crop, 2 ft. 6 in. (c. 75 cm.).

Distance apart of plants
Early, 12 in. (c. 30 cm.) Main crop, 15 in. (c. 35 cm.).

Shoots appear
In about 3 weeks (according to weather).

Ready to dig
Early kinds in mid summer.
Main crop from late summer.

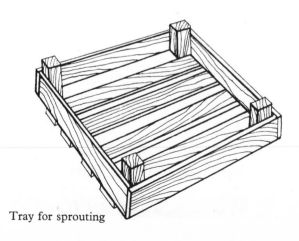

Tray for sprouting

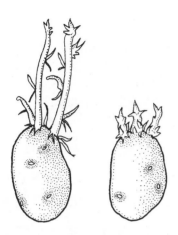

Incorrect   Correct

until planting time. Then the tray can be carried over to the potato patch without disturbing its load of sprouted seed. When planting, be very careful not to break the shoots, particularly when you cover the planting trench in again with soil.

Planting

Some people plant potatoes the lazy way by making holes with a large-sized dibber or thick stick and putting in the tubers. That is not a good idea, because some of the tubers may be left hanging with an air space beneath; if the air space becomes filled with water the tuber may rot, and if it doesn't the plant may suffer from lack of water. So it is best to dig out planting trenches about 5 inches deep and set the tubers firmly on the bottom. If you want to give the young plants a good start in life, and you do not think the manure or compost in the ground is enough, you can sprinkle some complete fertilizer (containing nitrogen, potash and phosphorus) into the trench at the rate of 2 or 3 ounces a yard and fork it lightly in before planting. Ask your local nurseryman to recommend the best varieties of potato to suit your soil and climate; not all varieties

to sprout in too dark a place, with the result that the shoots have grown long, pale and weak; they will probably get knocked off or squashed during planting, or even if they avoid that fate they will most likely shrivel and die back. From its appearance the tuber was kept in too warm a place as well. The combination of warmth and darkness is guaranteed to ruin even the best seed potato.

The right-hand drawing shows the results of correct sprouting in a light, cool place (though of course it must be frost-proof). The sprouts are plump, green, sturdy and short, so that they will not get damaged during planting. If more than four or five sprouts form on a tuber, rub off the weaker ones, and the ones that are left will grow all the stronger. The ideal size for a seed potato is about that of a good hen's egg. If you find any very large tubers you can cut them in half and so increase the number of plants and the amount of your crop. Never cut the tuber across; always cut it lengthwise, as shown in the drawing, so that each half has one or two good sprouts at the end.

Stand the tubers upright in the tray so that the sprouting buds are on top and leave them alone

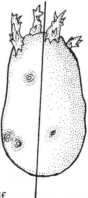

Cutting tuber in half

are suitable for all conditions, and even though it may seem expensive, try to obtain fresh certified seed every year. It will have been grown under the best conditions and inspected regularly to prevent pests and diseases. If in spite of that advice you decide you want to use seed saved from your own plants, use only the cleanest and healthiest-looking tubers, and even then do not use your own seed for more than one season; otherwise you may build up pests and diseases in the soil that will seriously affect crops in future years.

Care during growth

When the shoots appear above the ground you may hoe lightly between plants to remove weeds and freshen up the surface, but be careful not to damage any of the new shoots. If a sharp frost should threaten, it is a good plan to place a few inches of soil over the new growth, covering it completely. It is surprising how effective that few inches of earth can be in protecting the plants against spring frosts; the shoots will soon grow through the extra soil and you will have been spared the discouraging experience one frosty morning of finding the new growth blackened and dead.

'Earthing up'

When the plants are 8 inches or so high, the soil on each side of them should be drawn up nearly to the tops. The illustration will show why this rather tiresome operation is necessary. The potato plant has a natural tendency to send out underground runners, or stolons, from the original tuber, in all directions—downwards, sideways and even upwards. So some of the new potatoes that form on those stolons will grow above the surface of the ground and turn green; that will make them not only unattractive to eat but dangerous, because in those

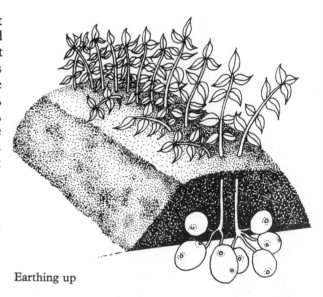

Earthing up

green tubers a chemical substance called solanine will develop which is a poison.

Another reason why earthing-up is a good idea is that the soil supports the top growth and prevents it from flopping about; this makes it much easier to walk between the rows when spraying time comes without trampling on the plants.

The best tool to use for earthing-up is the draw-hoe. Stand on one side of the row and draw up the soil on the other side. Do not make the sides of the ridge too steep, or some of the potatoes will poke out sideways and become exposed; they will then turn green and inedible and the purpose of the earthing-up will have been frustrated. A second earthing-up may be done three or four weeks after the first, the soil being drawn up three or four inches more. However, do not be too enthusiastic with your earthing-up. The plants have got to breathe, and the leaves cannot perform their proper functions if they keep getting covered with earth.

Potatoes

Lifting the crop

The first early potatoes can be dug in early to mid summer, according to variety, district and season, and how early they were planted. If you can't wait to eat some small new potatoes before your friends and neighbors, by all means dig up a plant or two while the tops are still growing and green—but remember the tubers will not have reached their best in size or flavor.

The proper time to lift your potato crop is when the leaves start to turn yellow. With early kinds this will probably be in late summer; with maincrop varieties in the fall. Choose a dry spell if at all possible; the crop will be cleaner and so will your boots. When digging up potatoes, take care to dig the fork into the ground a few inches away from the row, so that you do not spear any of the tubers. After lifting each plant, run the fork through the soil two or three more times to make sure no tubers get left behind. Pick out all potatoes that have been damaged or attacked by pests or disease. Badly affected ones should be removed and burned at once; less damaged ones can be put on one side for immediate use.

It is most important that potatoes should be thoroughly dry before being stored, otherwise they will almost certainly rot. For this reason, after they have been dug up they should be left on the ground, or if that is wet on a path, so that the sun can dry off their skins. Do not leave them too long, though, or they will turn green and uneatable.

Storing

Potatoes should be stored in a dark place free from damp and pests. It should be frost-proof but cool; if tubers are kept in the warm they will soon start sprouting and turn soft. If you have not sufficient storage space indoors or in a shed or garage, you can make a potato clamp, as shown in the drawing. Choose the highest part of your ground, so that rainwater will run away from it and not into it, and pile the tubers into a mound about 3 feet high and as long as necessary. Cover the tubers with a good thick layer of straw, and on this put a layer of soil 4 inches thick. If this soil is dug from a trench on each side of the clamp, that will provide excellent drainage. A tuft of straw should protrude through the covering of earth at intervals, to allow the potatoes to breathe. From time to time the stored tubers should be sorted through, and any that show signs of rotting or shriveling should be removed; otherwise they will infect the rest.

Pests and diseases

Unfortunately a great many pests and diseases attack the potato, probably more than any other vegetable.

COLORADO POTATO BEETLES, the yellow and black striped pest whose grubs can rapidly defoliate a plant, can be disposed of by spraying with sevin or malathion.

WIREWORMS can do great damage to the tubers, especially in newly cultivated ground. So can SLUGS, particularly in wet soil in the fall. Both these pests are dealt with in the section *Garden*

Potato clamp

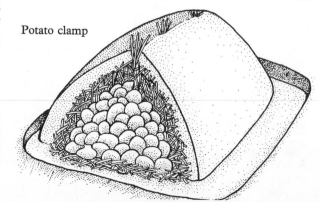

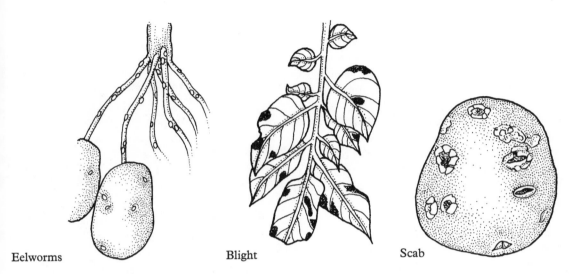

Eelworms   Blight   Scab

foes. The longer the potatoes are left in the ground the more they are liable to attack, so dig them up as soon as they are ready. EELWORMS are minute creatures that cause small cysts on the roots, as shown, and wreck the crop. The only way to avoid this trouble is to make sure you never grow potatoes on the same piece of ground two years running. Better still, as explained in the section *Rotation of crops*, grow potatoes so that they do not occupy the same piece of ground more than one year in three.

BLIGHT is the commonest and most destructive disease of potatoes; especially in wet seasons. Brown spots appear on the edges and tips of the leaves, as shown, quickly enlarge and spread to the stems, so that soon the plant becomes a blackened, foul-smelling mass. If this happens, the only thing to do is to cut off the stalks completely and take them away and burn them before digging up the crop; otherwise if left they will produce millions of spores of the blight fungus which will drop on to the soil and infect the tubers, turning them brown and horrible. Blight can best be controlled by covering the plants with a preventive spray of fungicide in July and again three weeks later; be careful to wet the under sides of the leaves as well as the tops. Bordeaux Mixture is widely used against blight, but there are newer and more effective sprays available.

SCAB is a common trouble that makes raised spots on the skin, as shown. Though only skin-deep they look very unattractive. If the soil has plenty of humus in it—from manure, compost, peat or even grass clippings—scab is unlikely to occur.

SUNSTROKE sometimes happens if the summer is very hot and dry. The stem shrivels at ground level and the plant collapses. Once again, plenty of humus in the soil will help, but the most important thing is to plant early enough, so that by the time the sun becomes fierce there are sufficient leaves to shade the base of the stem.

18. The cabbage family

ALL THE MEMBERS of this large and important family like rich, well-manured soil and particularly need a good supply of nitrogen. If given an excess of this, however, they tend to make soft, rank growth which is not firm or hardy enough to stand bad weather.

They will thrive on the heaviest of soils so long as it is well drained and not sour. If there is any deficiency of lime this should be made up, to protect against club root disease. The planting-out quarters should be *firm*. A good plan is to grow these vegetables in soil well manured for the previous crop, such as onions (see *Rotation of crops*).

All members of the cabbage family are transplanted from seed beds. You can raise hundreds of seedlings from a very small amount of seed. By juggling around with planting dates they can all be adapted to grow throughout the country, and they have a surprisingly long growing season.

Amount of seed required
A small packet will produce hundreds of plants.

When to sow
Spring cabbages in late summer. Summer and fall cabbages in mid spring. Winter cabbages in late spring.

Depth to sow
In ½-in. (c. 1 cm.) drills in a seed-bed.

Seedlings appear
In 8 or 9 days.

When to plant out
Spring cabbages in mid fall. Summer and fall cabbages in mid spring. Winter cabbages in mid summer.

Distance apart
Spring cabbages, 18 in. (c. 45 cm.). Others, 2 ft. (c. 60 cm.).

Ready to cut
Spring cabbages by late spring. Summer and fall cabbages, summer onwards. Winter cabbages, from late fall.

Spring cabbage

CABBAGES

Pictured here are three different types of cabbage: the spring variety, which is usually pointed; the round-headed summer and fall kind; and the crinkly-leaved winter kind (often called Savoy cabbage) which will stand up to very cold weather in the open. Except for different sowing and planting times all benefit from the same kind of treatment, and all unfortunately suffer from the same troubles.

Sowing

All cabbages are raised in a seed bed in short drills (some sow them in pots to avoid root damage when transplanting, but the slight gain is hardly worth the extra effort). If the weather is very dry, give the bed a good watering after sowing.

PROTECTION FROM BIRDS If birds are a nuisance, the seed bed may be protected from them by

Summer cabbage

Savoy cabbage

stretching black thread across it. When the birds swoop down to peck up the seed, the invisible threads snatch at them and scare them away. This and other ways of protecting against birds are shown in the section *Peas and beans*.

When the seedlings are well above the ground, they should be thinned if necessary, otherwise they may grow drawn and leggy and flop about when planting time comes. Do not leave the thinnings on the ground to attract pests; collect them as you go along and put them on the compost heap.

Transplanting

Spring cabbages should be planted in their final quarters in mid fall (a little earlier in cold districts). Do not put them in rich ground or give them any fertilizer, or they might make too much growth which will be too soft to stand harsh weather during the winter. They can, however, have some fertilizer sprinkled around them in the spring, to give them a boost when the cold weather is over. Spring sown cabbages may be planted out during the summer according to the variety and size of plants. The sooner this is done, the less the roots will be damaged and the sturdier the plants will be. For these summer plantings a light sprinkling of a complete fertilizer can be given to the soil around them, to help recovery and growth. In all cases, plant *firmly*.

In addition to the kinds of cabbage listed above, which need no protection, very early summer cabbages can be grown from a sowing under glass in late winter and planting out in the spring. If you have no glass, or cannot be bothered, plants may be bought.

There are also some excellent modern varieties of white cabbage which make very hard, round heads and which will keep very well throughout the winter; they are not only very good cooked but can be shredded up raw to make salads and coleslaw.

Hanging cabbage

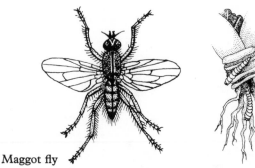

Maggot fly

They can be sown in the spring and planted out in the summer. Unfortunately if they are left outside during winter rain, ice, frost and snow they become slimy and revolting; but if they are pulled up by mid fall and hung up by the stalk, head downwards, as shown, in a shed or garage, they will remain perfect for months. Red cabbage may be treated in the same way, though it is somewhat **hardier** than the white kinds.

Pests and diseases
There are unfortunately quite a number of troubles to which cabbages are liable.

FLEA BEETLES   These tiny, black pests are a menace to cabbages in their seedling stage, puncturing and shredding the leaves so badly that they weaken the plants and may even kill them. Methods of control are the same as those given for radishes (which are closely related to cabbages) in the section *Root vegetables*.

CABBAGE WORMS   These are the larvae of the white butterfly. They feed on the leaves but can be controlled with diazinon or sevin.

CABBAGE LOOPER will also enjoy the leaves, so remove them before they can get to work.

CABBAGE MAGGOT FLY   This is really a dreadful pest. In badly infested areas its attacks can be so destruc-

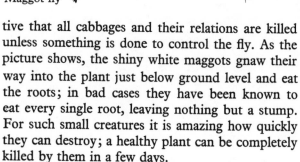

tive that all cabbages and their relations are killed unless something is done to control the fly. As the picture shows, the shiny white maggots gnaw their way into the plant just below ground level and eat the roots; in bad cases they have been known to eat every single root, leaving nothing but a stump. For such small creatures it is amazing how quickly they can destroy; a healthy plant can be completely killed by them in a few days.

Luckily some very powerful insecticides have at last been produced which control this pest extremely well. Dust the powder into the hole at planting time and then over the surface of the soil when the planting has been done. It has a double action: it repels the female flies so that they do not lay their eggs near it, and it kills any maggots that hatch out. Old-fashioned methods of control include sprinkling sand soaked in kerosene around the plants to put the flies off the scent, and placing a square of tar paper round the base of the plant as explained in the section *Natural pest control*.

CABBAGE APHIDS   This pest is common to all members of the cabbage family and is dealt with under *Cauliflower*.

CLUB ROOT   This is far the most serious disease to affect members of the cabbage family. It causes the roots to swell up and develop grotesque malformations which, as you can see here, distort them to such an extent that they are barely recognizable as roots at all. Club root is caused by an organism called a slime fungus which invades the plant tissues from the soil. Once inside, it multiplies so rapidly that at last the swollen roots burst, releasing a mass of evil-smelling slime to carry infection to other plants.

Once the disease has gained a hold there is no known cure. So as soon as you find an infected plant (above-ground symptoms include stunting, pale leaves and a sickly or dying look) dig it out before it has reached bursting point and *burn* it. Do not put it on the compost heap; the danger of infection is too great. Treat the ground from which the plant was dug with a good dressing of lime and *do not grow any cabbages or their relations on the same piece of land for at least three years*.

The disease can sometimes be prevented from infecting cabbages and the like by applying anti-club root fungicide to the seed bed before sowing and to the planting holes before transplanting.

Club root is prevalent only in soil that is deficient in lime, so make quite sure that there is enough lime in the ground before planting any of the cabbage family on it.

YELLOW BLIGHT Buy a resistant variety to this disease, caused by bacteria getting into the roots which makes the leaves wilt and turn yellow.

CAULIFLOWER
A tender vegetable that is sensitive to extremes of both cold and hot weather, so take this into account when deciding on the best time to grow it in your area and be sure to choose the most suitable variety.

Sowing
Sow spring-heading and fall-heading kinds in a seed bed and treat as advised under *Cabbage*. Summer-heading kinds may be sown indoors, or under glass (unheated) if you have a greenhouse or frame—or a friend with one and space in it to spare. If you have not, plants may be bought in spring.

Transplanting and cultivation
Methods, soil conditions and the use of fertilizers are the same as for *Cabbages*.

Protection
When the head starts to form on a cauliflower it is a good plan to place a broken leaf over it, as shown. This will keep it white by protecting it from rain, frost and sun, all of which can spoil and discolor it.

Club root

Breaking leaf

Cauliflower

Pests and diseases

These are the same as for *Cabbages*.

EARWIGS can also be a nuisance, infesting the heads and spoiling them. Sprays or dusts can be bought to get rid of these pests. If you are worried about using such lethal chemicals near to cutting time, try dealing with the earwigs as suggested in the section *Garden foes*.

CABBAGE APHID, shown here, is an unpleasant pest, gray in color, which forms colonies on members of the cabbage family and weakens them by sucking the sap. It is specially fond of cauliflowers because their incurving leaves make an ideal hiding place for it. To destroy this pest spraying must be very thorough so that every aphid in the colony gets wet.

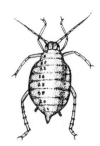

Cabbage aphid

Amount of seed required
A small packet will provide hundreds of plants.

When to sow
In most parts of the country cauliflower is best grown as a fall crop, sow in mid to late summer. In cool summer areas sow indoors in early spring.

Depth to sow
In ½-in. (c. 1 cm.) drills in a seed bed.

Seedlings appear
In about 9 days.

When to plant out
Mid to late spring for a summer crop, late summer for a fall crop.

Distance apart
2 ft. (c. 60 cm.) each way.

Ready to cut
Spring-heading, spring to early summer according to variety. Summer-heading, mid summer. Fall-heading, early fall to mid winter.

If you do not like using poison sprays, use one of those described in *Natural pest control*.

BROCCOLI

This is a delicious vegetable which produces large quantities of tender young flower shoots for picking over a period of several weeks. There are different kinds: green-sprouting broccoli (or calabrese) which crops in the fall, and the less common purple and white-sprouting alternatives. There is also a less recommended heading broccoli that is grown in a similar way to cauliflower.

Broccoli

Amount of seed required
A small packet will give hundreds of plants.

When to sow
Early spring. Or late fall if summers are hot and winters mild.

Depth to sow
In ½-in. (c. 1 cm.) drills in a seed bed.

Seedlings appear
In about 9 days.

When to plant out
Early to mid summer.

Distance apart
2 ft. (c. 60 cm.) each way.

Ready to pick
Late summer to early fall.

Sowing, planting and cultivation
Same as for *Cabbages*.

Pests and diseases
Same as *Cabbages* and *Cauliflower*.

BRUSSELS SPROUTS

Sowing, planting and cultivation
Same as for *Cabbages*. The secret of getting good sprouts is to start early and give the plants plenty of room. They must be planted on really *firm* ground, and the earth trodden well down round the base at planting time. Remember: *firm* planting makes *firm* sprouts; *loose* planting makes *loose* sprouts.

In early fall some of the lower leaves may be removed to force the growth into the sprouts. Do not overdo this; the plants should never be completely robbed of foliage. When sprouts form,

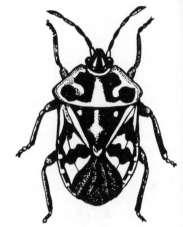

Harlequin bug

always pick off the lowest ones first and work your way up the plants during the picking period. If the lowest sprouts are flabby and unattractive, as they sometimes are, you should still pick them off.

They can be put on the compost heap if they do not look edible; never leave them on.

Pests and diseases
Same as for *Cabbages*.

HARLEQUIN or FIRE BUGS are one of the most destructive enemies of brussels sprouts, and other

Amount of seed required
A small packet gives hundreds of plants.

When to sow
Early to mid spring. Brussels will not grow well in the south.

Depth to sow
In ½-in. (c. 1 cm.) drills in a seed bed.

Seedlings appear
In about 9 days.

When to plant out
Early to mid summer.

Distance apart
2 ft. 6 in. (c. 75 cm.) each way.

Ready to pick
Early fall onwards.

members of the cabbage family, in the south half of the country. They suck the sap from the plants causing them to wilt and eventually die. The bugs are black with red markings and about $\frac{3}{8}$ inch long. They lay distinctive eggs that look like a double row of tiny white barrels each with a pair of black hoops. Hand picking is one of the most effective ways to control the pest, or use an insecticide such as rotenone.

KALE

It is almost unheard-of for kale to be damaged by frost; in fact many people say that frost improves the taste. It is always a good idea to have a few plants in your vegetable garden in case there should be a very cold winter that kills other greens. True, nobody could say that it has a great taste, but it does provide valuable greenstuff from mid winter to early spring when there is little else in the garden. The curled-leaf kind, something like parsley in appearance, even manages to look quite attractive in a dish.

Sowing, planting and cultivation
Same as for *Cabbages*.

Cutting
This should be done regularly, as soon as the shoots are of an edible size, so as to encourage the growth of plenty more young shoots. If you cannot make use yourself of all the greenstuff as it becomes ready, give it away to friends or put it on the compost heap. If left it will not only turn tough and bitter but will stop the formation of those tender new shoots that are the only reason for growing kale at all.

Pests and diseases
Same as for *Cabbages*.

Kale

Amount of seed required
A small packet gives hundreds of plants.

When to sow
Mid spring. (Or fall or winter for mild winter regions.)

Depth to sow
In $\frac{1}{2}$-in. (c. 1 cm.) drills in a seed-bed.

Seedlings appear
In about 9 days.

When to plant out
Early to mid summer.

Distance apart
2 ft. (c. 60 cm.) each way.

Ready to pick
Throughout the winter.

19. The spinach group

SPINACH is said to be one of the most health-giving of all vegetables, full of iron and vitamins and all kinds of other good things. In fact when it was first brought to Europe from Persia in the middle ages it was used entirely for medicinal purposes, because of its renown as the almost magical plant on which the mighty warriors of the Persian empire had built their legendary strength and endurance. Perhaps that is why small boys are still told by their parents that they will never grow up to be big strong men unless they eat up every last bit of their nice spinach. It is not a very easy vegetable to grow well; that is why some of its less difficult cousins are included with it in this section.

Spinach

Amount of seed required
½ oz. (c. 15 g.) will sow about 40 ft. (c. 12 m.).

When to sow
Summer spinach, early spring to mid summer. Winter spinach, late summer to early fall. Early spring spinach, in mild winter areas, sow in the fall.

Depth of drill
1 in. (c. 2.5 cm.).

Distance between rows
12 in. (c. 30 cm.).

Distance apart of plants
6 in. (c. 15 cm.).

Seedlings appear
In about 8 days.

Ready to pick
Summer spinach, early summer to mid fall. Winter spinach, late fall to mid spring.

SPINACH
Coming as it does from the eastern Mediterranean region, this vegetable might be expected to revel in hot, dry weather, and so in a way it does, because such conditions make it run quickly to seed, which is what nature intended it to do, instead of producing only leaves, which is what vegetable growers want it to do.

Soil and manuring
If spinach is to be prevented from shooting a seed stalk and becoming inedible, or as gardeners call it 'bolting', it must be grown on rich, moist land which never dries out. If you cannot give it such soil, if possible by adding plenty of manure or compost, do not bother to try to grow it because it will only make miserable little plants that are not worth the effort.

The best place to grow spinach, in fact, is not in the open but between rows of taller vegetables, which will shade the ground and so help to keep it moist.

Before sowing, you may give the ground a dressing of a complete fertilizer with a high proportion of nitrogen in it, because nitrogen stimulates the growth of large, juicy leaves.

Sowing
In the right moist soil, summer spinach grows very quickly, so the best way to sow it is a little at a time between other rows of vegetables every few weeks from mid spring to mid summer. The crop is mature within three months or so, and will therefore be picked and gone before the rows become crowded. Don't sow spinach to mature in hot weather—try one of the substitutes instead, especially New Zealand spinach or Swiss chard.

Care during growth
Keep rows of spinach free from weeds, which should not be allowed to compete with the crop for food and precious moisture.

THINNING should be carried out as soon as the seedlings are big enough to handle. Thin first to 3 inches apart; then when the leaves of neighbouring plants start to touch, every alternate one can be removed, leaving the remainder 6 inches apart. These last thinnings will be big enough to use.

Gathering
When the leaves have reached a good size, start picking them; if left they will become tough and bitter. Always pick the outer leaves and let the center ones remain to provide the next picking. Never remove more than half the leaves on a plant at one time, or you may kill it. When the plants have yielded their last picking, pull them up and put them on the compost heap.

FERTILIZER of a quick acting, high-nitrogen kind is often sprinkled lightly along the row after the first few pickings to keep up leaf production.

Protection
If really hard frosts threaten winter spinach, it is a good plan to protect the plants with straw or bracken to stop the leaves being spoiled and allow you to go on picking.

Pests and diseases
Running to seed is not exactly a disease but it is a nuisance. Avoid it by growing spinach in moist soil, and water if necessary, and omit sowings which would mature in hot weather.

CATERPILLARS of certain moths, such as the Cabbage Looper and Ermine Moth shown here, can develop a taste for spinach and eat the soft parts of the leaves away, leaving only a skeleton. Since spinach is used young, poison sprays are not advisable against these pests. Probably the best thing is to pick off the caterpillars and destroy them. If they hide themselves by day, look for them with a flashlight at night.

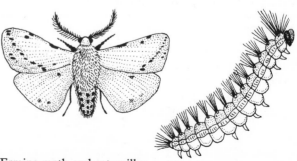

Ermine moth and caterpillar

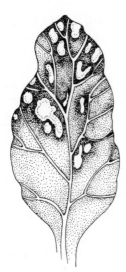

Downy mildew

MALABAR SPINACH

An excellent substitute for the 'real thing' which can, like spinach, be enjoyed cooked or raw. It grows quickly and can be trained to climb up a fence or trellis, thereby making it an excellent choice for gardeners with limited space. It will also grow well in hot weather without bolting.

SWISS CHARD

This very attractive vegetable is sometimes called seakale or leaf beet. It is a variety of beet with very broad, silvery white midribs to the leaves, and these midribs taste rather like asparagus if torn from the green part of the leaf and cooked separately; the green part itself tastes very like spinach. Swiss chard should be sown in mid spring or throughout the year if winters are mild.

The entire Swiss chard plant can be harvested by cutting it a couple of inches above the crown and new leaves will grow in its place. Or pick the outer leaves as you need them, leaving the center and remaining leaves to grow. Since chard is a warm weather plant it will continue to produce 'greens' throughout the summer, and will keep going through all but the most severe winters if the plants are protected by a deep layer of mulch, such as straw.

DOWNY MILDEW This is the commonest disease of spinach. Like most plant diseases it is caused by a fungus. As shown here, the leaves develop blotches, which may spread rapidly and do serious injury. These blotches are yellowish above and become covered with a violet-gray mealy or furry coating underneath. The best thing to do is to remove any affected leaves as soon as the disease is noticed.

Downy mildew is thought to be worst if the ground is at all waterlogged, so make sure that the soil, though moist, is well drained.

SPINACH BLIGHT Yellowing and mottling of the leaves is usually caused by a virus that is transmitted from one plant to another by insects. It usually occurs in warm summers, so if you live in such an area look for a resistant variety or grow one of the spinach substitutes.

NEW ZEALAND SPINACH

This is no relation to spinach at all, but comes from a completely different family of plants. Its taste is, however, not unlike that of spinach, for which it makes an excellent substitute.

Soil and manuring

New Zealand spinach will put up with the driest ground and the fiercest sun without ever running to seed.

Sowing

It cannot stand cold, so do not sow until frost is over. Since it makes a sprawling plant, allow 3 feet between rows and plants. Sow seeds in clusters of 3 or 4 and thin the seedlings to one in each place.

Care during growth

Keep the ground weeded regularly. Do not use fertilizer or the plants will get too big.

New Zealand spinach

Gathering

As soon as the leaves are big enough, pick them regularly until the plants are killed by the frost.

Pests and diseases

New Zealand spinach is remarkably trouble free.

Amount of seed required
½ oz. (c. 15 g.) will sow 50 ft. (c. 15 m.).

When to sow
Late spring.

Depth to sow
1 in. (c. 2.5 cm.).

Distance between plants
3 ft. (c. 90 cm.) each way.

Seedlings appear
In about 2 weeks.

Ready to gather
Late summer to mid fall.

Swiss chard

20. Onions and their relatives

NOBODY KNOWS how long onions and their kind have been grown for human food. They must have been cultivated in ancient Egypt, because when the hungry Israelites were on their long journey across the wilderness to the promised land they grumbled that they were sick of living on this strange new manna from heaven and longed to get back to the 'leeks, onions and garlic' they had learned to enjoy in captivity.

Certainly there is no plant family of more importance to our diet. The physicians of ancient times believed they had almost magical healing powers. Onion-laden breath has been known to kill romance, but modern scientists have discovered that it also kills practically all known germs. It is said by some that peas and beans strongly object to the onion family as neighbors, and that the dislike is mutual.

Globe onions

ONIONS
There are two basic shapes of onion—globe and flat—and three colors—white, yellow and red. Some prefer one kind and some the other, just as some prefer mild-flavored and some strong-tasting ones. All are grown in the same way.

Growing from seed
Also there are two different ways of growing onions—from seeds and from sets (i.e., small bulbs). Since growing from seed is the traditional—and indeed the natural—way, we will deal with that first.

Soil and manuring
Choose an unshaded site if possible. Coming as it does from the middle east, the onion likes as much sunshine as it can get. The most important thing is that the ground should be as rich as possible. Plenty of manure or good compost should have been dug in and well mixed with the soil. Firm ground is also essential to success with onions, so tread the earth down thoroughly before preparing the surface. This should then be raked to as fine a condition as possible, and all stones removed. A *complete*

Amount of seed required
¼ oz. (c. 7 g.) will sow 50 ft. (c. 15 m.).

When to sow
For main crop, early spring. For early crop, late summer.

Depth of drill
½ in. (c. 1 cm.).

Distance between rows
12 in. (c. 30 cm.).

Distance apart of plants
6 in. (c. 15 cm.).

Seedlings appear
In 2–3 weeks.

Full grown
Early crop in mid summer. Main crop in late summer or early fall.

Flat onions

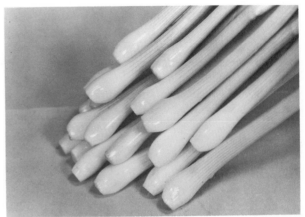

Green onions or scallions

fertilizer sprinkled on the soil and raked in before sowing will be a help, because onions are very heavy feeders.

Sowing

To make the biggest, firmest and longest-keeping bulbs, onions should have grown as large as possible before late spring, because that is the time when the longer days cause them to stop making new leaf growth and put all their energy into forming bulbs instead. So it is vital to sow the main crop just as early as you can. Try to do so as soon as the ground is dry enough to be raked to a fine surface. This will rarely be before early spring, but if it can be done in late winter so much the better.

Make the drills half an inch deep, and sow the seed as thinly as you possibly can along them. Thin sowing is important not just because it saves seed but because it also saves thinning and so avoids attracting the destructive onion maggot: the flies can smell thinned-out plants from a long way off and find the smell irresistible.

After sowing, cover the seeds over with the earth from the drill and tread it down as firmly as you can. Finish off by raking the surface smooth; rake along the row, not across it, to avoid getting the seed out of line. A sprinkling of a pesticide against onion maggot may be raked in at the same time.

For an early crop (and to lessen the chances of attack by the onion maggot, whose days are over by the fall) seed may be sown in late summer, in exactly the same way but rather more thickly. The plants from this sowing can either be transplanted in early spring or left to mature where they are. Some new kinds of early-maturing yellow-skinned onions developed in Japan are particularly good for this late summer sowing.

Care during growth

Since onions take some weeks to germinate and grow slowly in the early stages, weeds should be removed as soon as they appear, either by hand-pulling or by careful hoeing (but mind you do no damage to the onion plants, or they will give off that crushed-onion smell that is so enticing to the onion maggot fly.

THINNING The soil should be moist when this operation is performed. If it is not, water it first. Thin in two stages—first to an inch or two apart and then to the final distance of about 6 inches, by which time the thinnings will be big enough plants to be used as nice, juicy green onions in salads or with cheese. Never leave thinnings lying about (they attract the onion maggot), and always make the soil firm afterwards.

Growing by sets

The later stages of the growing and harvesting of onions are the same whether they are raised from seed or not, so we will now deal with the second way of growing onions, by sets.

Onion sets are modern inventions produced by controlled scientific methods, and represent a triumph of technology over nature. They have been treated by highly artificial techniques which have held them while still very young in a state of suspended growth. When planted out, however, they start growing again as if nothing had happened. They are less likely than ones raised from seed to be attacked by onion maggot or disease.

Quantity of sets required
½ lb. (c. 225 g.) to about 40 ft. (c. 12 m.).

When to plant
Early spring, or in the fall if conditions are favorable for winter growing.

Distance between rows
12 in. (c. 30 cm.).

Distance apart of sets
6 in. (c. 15 cm.).

Sprouting starts
In about 2 weeks.

Full grown
Late summer.

Soil and manuring
Exactly as for growing from seed.

Planting
Though onions should grow *on* the ground rather than in it, the sets should be pressed into the soil firmly, neck upright, so that they do not fall over and get a bad start in life. If birds are a nuisance and pull them up, protect the sets by means of wire netting or black thread (as shown under *Peas*) until they are fully rooted. Summer-sown onions may also be transplanted in early spring, unless you prefer to leave them to mature where they were sown, thinning out the surplus plants for use as green onions. When transplanting, the roots should be carefully dug up to avoid damage and planted into wide holes in which the roots are well spread out. Firm the soil well round them with your heel.

Care during growth
Continue weeding. If the ground becomes very dry, water the plants while they are young; later the roots should grow far enough down to find all the water they need.

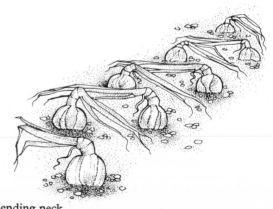

Bending neck

If any flower stems appear (they are tall and stiff, and carry a knob on top which if left will become a flowerhead) break them off as soon as you see them and remove them to the compost heap; if left they will take energy that should be going into the bulb.

Harvesting

When the onions are beginning to ripen the leaves will start turning yellow and falling sideways. You can help matters by bending the necks right down to the ground, as shown here. This will hasten ripening. At the same time many people lever up the plants with a garden fork until they hear the roots snap; this is thought to help the bulbs to harden and ripen by stopping further growth.

Leave the plants for two weeks longer and then lift them carefully on a dry day and lay them out on the ground so that the sun can get at them for a day or two longer. Any that show signs of rot should be removed. Thick-necked ones will not keep well, and should therefore be put aside for immediate use. When the bulbs are thoroughly ripe and the tops dry and papery, the onions should be stored in a rainproof and frost proof place to be used through-

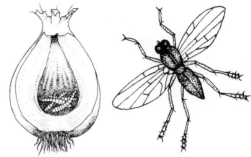

Onion maggot

out the winter and spring until next year's crop begins. To prevent rotting in store, air should be allowed to circulate freely round them. A good way to do this is to hang them up, either in net bags or strung together in ropes, as shown.

Pests and diseases

Certain troubles can spoil onions both during growth and in store. The commonest are listed here:

ONION MAGGOT   This very destructive pest, pictured here, has already been mentioned several times. The fly lays its eggs in the soil next to the growing plants in the spring. In a few days the grubs hatch out, bore their way into the base of the plant and eat away the middle. Affected plants turn yellow and shrivel; if you pull them up you will find fat white maggots inside them.

Spring-sown onions growing in northern states are most likely to be attacked by the fly, which is such a serious pest that a whole crop can be wiped out in a few days. In badly infested areas the best thing to do is to sow in late summer or to plant sets.

Once the maggot has got into a plant it is too late to do anything but pull up the plant and burn it. All efforts must therefore be directed at prevention, by the methods described in *Sowing*, *Thinning* and

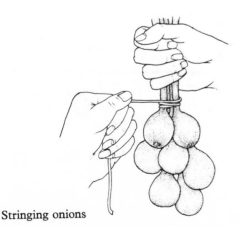

Stringing onions

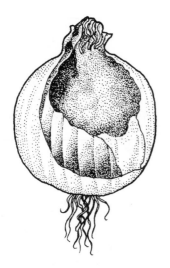

Neck rot

Planting above. If you object to the use of poisonous pesticides, you can try growing onions and carrots in alternate rows, as explained in the section *Natural Pest Control*.

NECK ROT   This disease starts where the tops join the bulbs and spreads rapidly through the flesh, so that infected onions soon become a soft, foul-smelling mess. Neck rot can attack the growing crop but more often attacks onions in store. Once the disease is seen, there is nothing to do but remove and destroy all infected onions before the trouble spreads.

WHITE ROT   See under *Garlic*.

ONION THRIPS   Small, yellow insects that feed on the juices in the leaves, causing them to whiten, wither and fall to the ground. They can also attack bulbs in storage. Control with malathion or a rotenone spray.

SHALLOTS

These mild-tasting members of the onion family are grown for eating raw or cooked, or for pickling. They grow in clumps of small bulbs, which should be split apart and planted separately, in rows 9 inches apart and with 6 inches between bulbs, in exactly the same way as *Onion sets*. Plant early, if possible in late winter. One pound will plant about 12 feet.

Harvesting
The bulbs will grow into clumps of 8–12, and should be lifted when the tops turn yellow in mid summer. Divide up the clumps and let the bulbs dry thoroughly; they can then be stored.

Pests and diseases
Same as for *Onions*, though maggot attacks are not serious. The following trouble also occurs:

SUN SCALD   Very hot sun before the bulbs are shaded by foliage may cause discolored, sunken patches, as shown. They have literally been baked.

Shallots

Sunscald

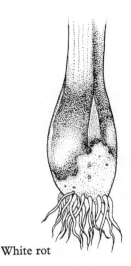

White rot

Smut

The trouble may be avoided by planting as early as possible, so that there are plenty of leaves before the sun becomes fierce.

GARLIC

This close relative of the onion is quite easy to grow, but since it grows under the surface of the ground it needs rather lighter soil than onions; some sand in the planting holes will help.

One pound of garlic will plant a row of about

Garlic

25 feet. Split up the clumps and plant the small bulbs, or 'cloves', in early spring like *Onion sets*, or in the fall in the south and southwest, but bury them completely.

Harvesting

Same as *Shallots*.

Pests and diseases

As for *Onions*. One disease that sometimes affects onions, but can be a much worse scourge of garlic, is the following:

WHITE ROT   This is a destructive fungus that forms, as shown, white furry patches which spread quickly, turning the plant into evil-smelling slime. Remove all affected plants immediately. Wet conditions encourage White Rot, so plant only in well-drained ground.

SMUT can invade the leaves, causing dirty-looking stripes which then go down into the bulb and cause it to rot. Remove affected plants at once.

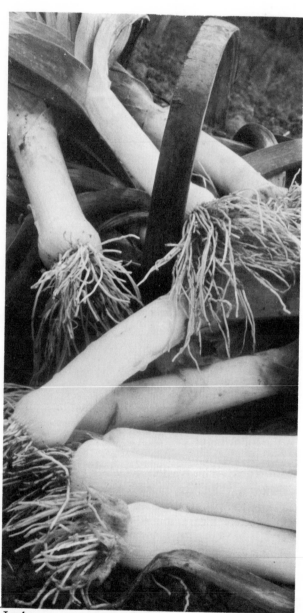

Leeks

LEEKS
There can hardly be a vegetable more passionately loved by some people and hated by others. Well-grown leeks are among the most nutritious vegetables, and the hardiest too.

Sowing
Prepare a seed bed by raking the soil to a fine surface. Draw the drill ½ inch deep; after sowing thinly along this, cover with soil, tread firmly and rake.

Care of seedlings
Weeding should be done to keep the tiny young seedlings from being choked. *Thinning* should not be needed unless you sowed much too thickly. *Watering* may be necessary in the very early stages if the weather is dry.

Transplanting
Do not transplant the seedlings until they are 6 inches high, in early or mid summer. If they are slightly overcrowded and somewhat drawn, so much the better. Some people plant in wide holes made with a trowel, spread out the roots carefully, and gently fill in with earth so as not to damage them. A much easier way is to make holes 6 inches deep with a dibber or blunt stick, and drop a seedling into each so that only its tip shows, as pictured here. Do not bother about filling in any soil; simply pour some water into each hole after planting and leave it at that. The young plants will have so much energy of growth in them that they will soon send down strong new roots and send up vigorous new leaves, and when digging time comes you will find 6 inches of sweet, juicy white 'stem' (leaf bases actually) where the planting hole was. This is the part that matters, so the longer it is the better.

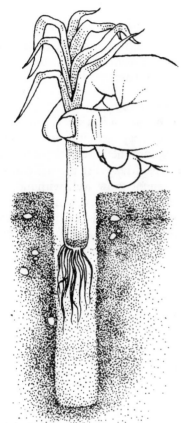

Planting leek in hole

Soil and manuring

The ground for growing leeks can be much the same as for *Onions*, but need not be so rich. Soil that was manured for a previous crop is quite suitable. It should be reasonably well drained, because the leeks are going to be there for a long time during wet weather and if they are standing in water they may rot.

Care during growth

Keep the plants weeded. A general fertilizer may be applied to the soil a week or two after transplanting to stimulate growth.

EARTHING UP is done by some people to give a few more inches of white stem, but is hardly worthwhile if the planting was done in holes, as explained above.

Pests and diseases

Same as for *Onions*, but leeks are remarkably trouble free.

Gathering

Do not try to pull leeks up by hand; they may snap. Lever them up gently with a fork. Leeks are among the hardiest of all vegetables and will stand through the winter without protection, ready for digging as you require them.

Amount of seed required
¼ oz. (c. 7 g.) will give hundreds of plants.

When to sow
Early to mid spring.

Depth to sow
In ½-in. (c. 1 cm.) drills, in a seed-bed.

Seedlings appear
In about 2 weeks.

When to plant out
Early to mid summer.

Distance between rows
12 in. (c. 30 cm.).

Distance apart of plants
9 in. (c. 23 cm.).

Ready to dig
Late fall to mid spring.

21. Peas and beans

THERE ARE many different kinds of both of these vegetables but they all have one thing in common. As members of the same large family, called *Legumes*, they have the remarkable property of being able to extract their own nitrogen from the air instead of having to have it ready provided for them in the soil like other plants.

This is because their roots carry swellings on them, called nodules, which look as if the plants were infected with some disease. They are in fact infected, but not with a disease. Each of those swollen nodules contains millions of bacteria which have the strange ability to take the nitrogen from the air, pass it through their bodies, and turn it into important plant foods known as *nitrates*. That is why, as explained in the section *Rotation of crops*, peas and beans will not only grow in nitrogen-starved soil but will add nitrogen to it themselves, to the benefit of the next crop to occupy that ground.

The fact that peas and beans provide their own nitrogen does not mean that they can do without other plant foods—far from it. They have a great deal of action to crowd into a very short life—germinating, growing, flowering and making fruits and seed—so they use up more energy than any other crop, and that takes plenty of nourishment. So the soil should be rich in plant foods. It must be well drained, but should contain plenty of moisture-holding material; dryness at the roots causes a poor crop and encourages the crippling disease called mildew.

PEAS

There are two main types of pea—the round-seeded kind and the wrinkled-seeded kind. Everyone agrees that the wrinkled ones are much better to eat and give much heavier crops than the round ones. But the round ones are much hardier, and so can, in favorable conditions, be sown in the fall to give early crops the following year. Wrinkled ones cannot safely be sown until the spring, except in the south and Pacific southwest, because they cannot stand winter cold and damp.

Soil and manuring

Peas should be grown in rich, deep soil, so that the roots can go deep to find food and moisture. Compost dug into the lower part of the topsoil gives ideal conditions. Make sure the soil contains enough lime; peas cannot grow well without it. Nitrogen, as explained before, is not necessary, but there should be plenty of nourishment in the soil, because peas are greedy feeders. Apply a light dressing of a complete fertilizer just before sowing time.

Sowing

The best way to sow peas is in a drill drawn about 3 inches deep *with the whole width of the hoe*. Sow the seeds about 2–3 inches apart, as shown, the

---

Amount of seed required
½ lb. (c. 225 g.) to 30 ft. (c. 9 m.) row.

When to sow
Hardy (round-seeded), late fall. Early, early spring. Mid-season, mid spring. Late, late spring except where summers are hot.

Depth of drill
3 in. (c. 7.5 cm.).

Distance between rows
Dwarf, 18 in. (c. 45 cm.). Medium, 2–3½ ft. (c. 60–100 cm.). Tall, 4–5 ft. (c. 1.20–1.50 m.).

Distance apart of seeds
2–3 in. (c. 5–7 cm.), in wide drill.

Shoots appear
In about 10 days.

Ready to pick
Fall-sown, late spring. Early, early summer. Mid-season, mid summer. Late, late summer.

Peas

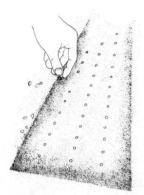

Sowing in a flat drill

Stretching thread

whole width of the drill, as evenly as possible. Allow half a pound to 30 feet of row. Mice can be a great nuisance, carrying the seeds away to their nest and eating them, or feeding them as a great delicacy to their hungry young. To discourage such raids, many people soak the seeds in kerosene before sowing them, to make them unpalatable to the mice.

After sowing the seed, cover in the drill with soil again. Firm the soil by *lightly* treading it and finish by raking it to an even surface.

A fall sowing of a round-seeded hardy variety is not really worth while in districts where the ground gets very wet and frozen in the winter, but in suitable districts it will give you pickings of peas several weeks before the spring-sown ones. To ensure good drainage, drills for these fall sowings may be shallower than those for spring sowings. Sowing at intervals throughout the spring will give you a succession of peas throughout the summer. Some people sow any seed still left in early summer, to give pickings early in the fall.

Birds can do a great deal of damage to newly-sown rows of peas, and unfortunately, they do not have the same sense of smell as mice do, so kerosene does not deter them. However, they can be kept at bay by covering the row with wire-netting, or stretching black thread, fixed to sticks, two or three inches above the ground, as shown. As a general rule, *the distance between rows of peas should be the same as the height of the pea*; if planted much closer, they will not make such good growth or give such a good crop.

This means, of course, that tall varieties of peas will take up a good deal of ground, and for that reason many people grow only dwarf kinds. However, there is just as much time and effort needed to grow dwarf peas as tall ones, but the tall ones give a much bigger crop, so grow some if you can possibly spare the space. In any case the plants will only occupy the ground for three months, from the time of sowing to the time the last pod is picked.

Care during growth

When the young green shoots are well above the ground, pull out any weeds that appear among them if you can spare the time; unfortunately the right conditions for growing peas are also ones that encourage the growth of the most robust weeds.

STAKING should be done when the plants are 3 or 4 inches above the ground. If they are allowed to get taller they will flop about and the job will be made much more difficult. Do not believe the seed packet that says that the pea it contains does not need staking. All peas, no matter how dwarf, are the better for support; nature gave them tendrils because they were intended to be climbing plants. Choose twiggy sticks 18 inches higher than the height to which it says on the packet that the pea will grow. Drive the sticks well into the ground so that they are firm enough to stand up to strong winds; a row of peas in full growth presents as much wind-resistance as a ship in full sail. Many people nowadays use netting strung on stakes to support their peas, but it is much more difficult to avoid wind damage by this method.

Set the sticks 6 inches apart along each side of the row, as shown, at such an angle that they meet in the middle above it. If possible, push smaller twigs into the ground between the sticks. These will help the plants to climb in their early stages. If possible, *use fresh sticks each season.* Last year's sticks not only snap very easily but may be infested with all kinds of pests which winter in them.

EARTHING-UP When the plants are well up the sticks, it is a good plan to draw up the earth an inch or two high on each side of the row by means of the hoe. This ridged-up earth will give extra support and will act as a mulch during dry weather, preventing the moisture from escaping from the ground.

Pests and diseases

Naturally a vegetable that is found so delicious by human beings is also thoroughly enjoyed by a great many pests. In addition, it is susceptible to disease.

MILDEW This is a fungus disease which in some years does a great deal of damage to peas. It is worst in very dry or very wet seasons; the reason is that mildew is encouraged both by a moist atmosphere, which keeps the leaves damp, and by dryness at the roots. The symptoms are unmistakable. White powdery patches appear on the leaves, as shown here; these enlarge, spread to other leaves and in bad cases infect the pods so that the whole plant becomes sickly and the crop is spoiled.

Staking

Mildew

Foot rot

If conditions are not too bad, and the disease is taken in hand early enough, mildew can be controlled by thorough spraying of the plants with a fungicide designed for the purpose. It is no use just asking for a fungicide, though, because not all of them are effective against this disease, so make sure you get a product that is recommended against powdery mildew.

If you live in a very dry place, it is really a waste of time to try to grow late peas, because whatever you do they will probably get mildew. In such conditions do not sow peas after late spring.

FOOT ROT This fungus attacks plants at soil level and just below. The stem, as shown, becomes sunken and blackened; the plant, having no support, shrivels from the roots upwards, wilts and dies. By the time the disease shows itself, it is too far gone to be cured, so the only thing to do is to pull up all infected plants and burn them.

Fortunately, foot rot is not much of a problem where the soil is in the right condition. It generally attacks peas only in *sour* soil—that is, soil that is badly drained and does not contain enough lime.

So if you should have your peas attacked by this disease, make sure next time that you grow them in soil that has been well dug and drained, and see to it that enough lime is added to stop the disease occurring again.

PEA MOTH You must have come across these whitish maggots, shown here, gnawing away the peas inside an innocent looking pod. You probably wondered how they could possibly have got there. The answer is that they are the grubs of an all-too-common species of moth which lays her eggs in the flowers just when the pods are beginning to form. As the eggs hatch out the tiny maggots make their way into the embryo pod and proceed to gorge themselves and grow fat inside it by eating their way through the developing peas as the pod swells. There used to be no effective way to stop this happening, so that in districts where there was a large population of pea moths it was almost impossible to find a pea-pod that did not contain one or two wriggling maggots. Now, fortunately, there are some highly effective sprays on the market which if used immediately flowering is over will almost completely prevent the trouble.

THRIPS If you find blossoms fading and dropping right off the plant as if they had been cut off with scissors, thrips have probably been at work. They are the tiny dark creatures pictured here which are

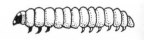

Pea moth and grub

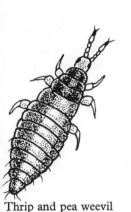
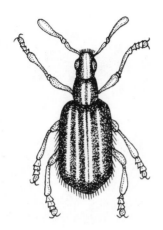

Thrip and pea weevil

the plant like a stone and lie on the ground as if dead. They weaken the plants if they gnaw them very much, but they do not usually form a major pest on peas. If they seem to be getting out of hand, an insecticide spray will reduce their numbers.

MILLIPEDES There are several species of these objectionable creatures, of which the commonest is pictured here. They are sluggish in their habits (not fast-moving like the friendly centipede) and curl up into a flat spiral if threatened. They live in the soil, and if there is a bad infestation of them they can do very great damage indeed, by eating the seed as soon as it is sown and before it has time to germinate. They are also quite capable of gnawing their way into growing plants and destroying the roots. They are difficult if not impossible to get rid of completely, but they can be controlled effectively if the ground is treated with a soil pesticide before the seed is sown. The pesticides that control them are the same sort that are used against wireworms (see the section *Garden foes*).

often called thunder flies and sometimes appear in large numbers in warm weather, attacking a wide range of plants, and not only their flowers but their leaves which become mottled and sickly. Sprays can also be bought which will control this little pest.

If your peas are badly attacked you should make certain that next year's peas and beans are grown as far away as possible, and as soon as the crop has been gathered take the pea sticks away and burn them to prevent them from becoming hiding places from which the thrips can launch a new attack in the following season.

PEA WEEVILS These small creatures often appear in early summer, especially in the western states, and nibble holes in the leaves. If disturbed they drop off

Picking
Start picking the pods as soon as they fill out (you can tell by pressing them gently between finger and thumb) and continue throughout the season. Be careful not to miss any. This constant removal of pods stimulates the formation of new ones.

When the row is exhausted, pull up the plants and put them on the compost heap.

BUSH BROAD BEANS, OR FAVA
Like peas, these can be sown in the fall and the spring, but they are a good deal hardier and able to stand harder winters. It is a European favorite that is often chosen as a substitute for the Lima bean in the northern states.

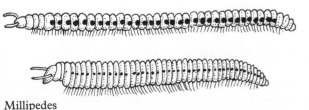

Millipedes

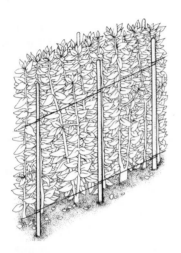

Staking

Soil and manuring
Same as for *Peas*.

Sowing
If your site is warm and well drained, you can make a sowing in late fall; this will give a very early crop. If your site is cold, however, the crop will do

---

Amount of seed required
¼ lb. (c. 112 g.) to 25 ft. (c. 7.50 m.) row.

When to sow
Late fall and early spring.

Depth to sow
3 in. (c. 7.5 cm.).

Distance between rows
3 ft. (c. 90 cm.).

Shoots appear
In about 2 weeks.

Ready to pick
Fall-sown in early summer. Spring-sown in mid summer.

Bush beans, or fava

so badly that fall sowing is not worthwhile. The main sowing is made in late winter or early spring, according to the condition of the soil. Sow seeds 6 inches apart in a double row, zigzag fashion, in a wide drill.

Care during growth
Keep the ground weeded. Since broad beans grow quite tall and have large leaves, they can be flattened by wind and rain if they are not supported. The picture shows a good way to do this, by driving in stout stakes at intervals on both sides of the row and stretching strong cord between them so that it completely encircles the row of plants.

Pests and diseases
Most of the troubles that affect broad beans are the same as those described under *Peas*. However, broad beans suffer particularly from the following troubles.

BLACK BEAN APHID This is a particularly nasty form of aphid which has a special liking for beans. If not controlled it can so badly infest the growing shoots as to cripple them completely, as shown; it

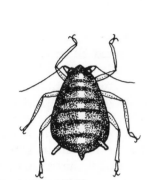

Black bean aphid

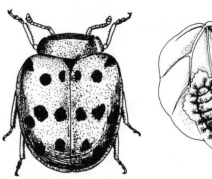

Mexican bean beetle

can spread to the pods and make them unusable. Fall-sown beans are not often badly attacked. The best way to prevent the spring sown ones from becoming infested is to pick off the growing tips of the plants as soon as the first beans start to form. If in spite of this some aphids appear, they can be destroyed by spraying with rotenone or malathion.

MEXICAN BEAN BEETLE A brown with black spots enemy of different types of beans that feeds on the leaves. Crush its yellow egg clusters before they hatch, hand pick the beetles and use a rotenone spray.

Picking
See *Peas*.

LIMA BEANS

A warm weather crop that requires a long growing season with relatively high temperatures. If the conditions are suitable grow either the low growing bush varieties or the tall growing pole varieties that need to be supported.

POLE BEANS

Properly grown, these can be among the most prolific of all vegetables, giving an enormous return for comparatively little seed and effort. Lots of different varieties to choose from, including scarlet flowered runner beans.

Soil and manuring
Same as for *Peas*.

Amount of seed required
¼ lb. (c. 225 g.) to 40 ft. (c. 12 m.) row.

When to sow
Mid to late spring (depending on the variety and climate).

Depth to sow
2–3 in. (c. 5.0–7.5 cm.)

Distance between rows
4–6 ft. (c. 1.20–1.80 m.)

Distance apart of seed
8 in. (c. 20 cm.).

Shoots appear
In about 10 days.

Ready to pick
From mid summer onwards.

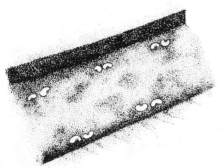

Sowing

Sowing

Since most beans are warm season crops, they should not be sown until the soil has warmed up; in favorable places this may be mid spring, in cold places late spring.

The best way to sow is in a zigzag double row, the seeds being planted 2–3 inches deep and 6–8 inches apart. Not every one will germinate or make a strong plant, so a good way to sow is as pictured: seeds are sown in pairs at each side of a wide drill, and when the plants come up each pair is thinned so as to leave only the strongest.

Staking

Care during growth

Remove all weeds, particularly in the early stages before the plants are in full growth.

STAKING It is best to stake pole beans at the time of sowing. The poles should be strong ones, 8 feet long, and one should be allowed to each plant. Drive each stake well into the ground until they are quite firm. Since they are going to have to withstand a great deal of wind, they should be made as strong as possible. A very good way to do this is to fasten horizontal cross-poles along the row about three-quarters of the way up the stakes, as shown, and tie them with strong twine or cord, so that the structure looks like an elongated teepee.

When training beans it is worth remembering that *they always twine themselves in the opposite way to the apparent movement of the sun.* If, to give them a helping hand, you twist them round their poles in the wrong direction you will have wasted your time, because they will only unwind themselves again.

Pests and diseases

Same as for *Peas* and *Broad Beans*.

Picking

See *Peas*. The essential difference between snap beans and Lima or broad beans is that the former are not shelled before they are eaten. So, it is particularly important that the pods should be picked while they are still young and tender. If left a few days too long they will become stringy and the skin will turn so tough that it will defy the strongest teeth.

BUSH SNAP BEANS

One of the best choices for the home garden, especially where space is limited. They are warm season plants but can be grown throughout most of the country.

Amount of seed required
¼ lb. (c. 112 g.) to 50 ft. (c. 15 m.) run.

When to sow
Mid to late spring. In the lower south and south west they can be sown in the fall.

Depth of drill
3 in. (c. 7.5 cm.).

Distance between rows
3 ft. (c. 90 cm.).

Distance apart of seeds
6 in. (c. 15 cm.).

Shoots appear
In about 2 weeks.

Ready to pick
From mid summer onwards.

Soil and manuring
Same as for *Peas*.

Sowing
Bush beans are also usually sown in a zigzag double row, with the seeds planted 3 inches deep and 6 inches apart.

Dwarf bean

Care during growth
Same as for *Peas*.

Pests and diseases
Many of the troubles that attack *Peas* and *Broad Beans* can be a nuisance. There are two diseases that seem to prefer snap beans, however.

HALO BLIGHT As the name implies, and as the picture shows, this disease announces its presence by forming circular patches with a halo effect at the edges. Affected pods should be removed. Mildly affected ones can be used; the rest should be burned. The disease seems worst in sour soil.

ANTHRACNOSE This, as pictured, shows itself by characteristic markings. It can spoil the pods and the plants as a whole, and is thought to be encouraged by poor growth and nutritional deficiencies. So make sure that the soil is in good condition and well fertilized.

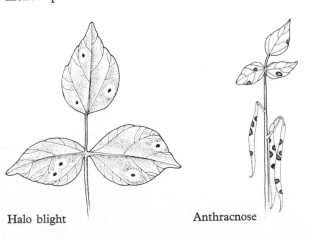

Halo blight   Anthracnose

22. Root vegetables

ALL ROOT vegetables do best in light soil, so if your soil is heavy it should have been lightened and put into better condition by the methods explained in the section *Improving the soil*. Above all, the ground must be well drained.

As explained in the section *Rotation of crops*, root vegetables should not be grown in freshly manured ground. The reason is shown below under carrots.

CARROTS

There are three main kinds of carrot. The short, or stump-rooted, grow quickest and are the first to be sown for an early crop. The medium rooted, or intermediate, are usually sown a little later; some are pulled for use while still young and sweet, and the rest are left to mature. The long-rooted varieties are grown more for the eye than for the palate; they tend to be coarse both in texture and in taste.

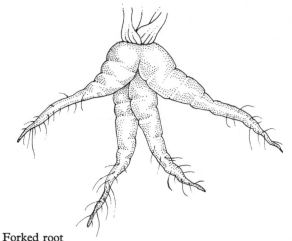

Forked root

Amount of seed required
¼ oz. (c. 7 g.) will sow 50 ft. (c. 15 m.).

When to sow
Earlies in early spring. Main crop in mid to late spring. A late sowing may be made in early summer, if summer is not too hot, and fall in mild winter areas.

Depth of drill
1 in. (c. 2.5 cm.).

Distance between rows
Short-rooted, 9 in. (c. 23 cm.). Intermediate, 12 in. (c. 30 cm.). Long, 15 in. (c. 38 cm.).

Seedlings appear
In 2–3 weeks.

Ready to gather
Earlies in mid to late summer. Main crop in early to mid fall. Late crop should be lifted by late fall.

Soil and manuring

Carrots prefer a light soil, or one that has been lightened by being thoroughly cultivated. It must be well drained. Never grow them on freshly manured ground. If you do, they have no incentive to grow straight down in search of moisture and food, because they can get it more easily by branching sideways, and so the roots become forked and stringy, as shown here. On the other hand, carrots will not grow well in land that lacks nourishment. It is a good plan, therefore, to sprinkle a dressing of a complete fertilizer on the surface and rake it in a few days before sowing the seed.

Sowing

Carrot seeds are small, and need a finely raked surface to give them the best start in life. Draw the sowing drill about 1 inch deep. If carrot rust fly is a nuisance in your district, and you do not object to the use of poisonous chemicals, sprinkle a powder against soil-pests along the drill; if you dislike poisons you can try growing onions alongside your

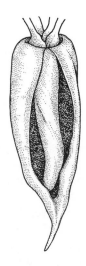

Splitting root

the roots start growing again they cannot expand except by bursting their skins and the result is that the roots split, as shown here. So try to keep enough moisture in the ground to stop this from happening, by watering if necessary.

THINNING   If the seeds were sown thinly enough, no further thinning should be necessary until the plants begin to crowd each other, by which time the roots will be big enough to use. From then on, thinning can be carried out as and when carrots are required. The plants that are left to mature will then be the right final distance apart. The ground should be well firmed down after thinning and all the thinnings should be removed (either being used or,

carrots, (see *Natural pest control*), or you may like to see whether you can keep the fly at bay by sowing scorzonera between the carrots as explained later in this section under *Scorzonera*.

Sow the seed thinly, tread the soil down firmly as you cover in the drill and finish with a light raking. Many people who like to eat carrots while still young and tender do not sow a whole row at a time but half a row every three weeks from mid spring until early summer, so that they can pull young roots in succession over several months.

Care during growth

Because carrots take some time to germinate and are slow-growing in their early stages, they can easily be choked by weeds. It is important, therefore, to keep the ground well weeded right from the start. The earliest carrots are sown while the soil still contains plenty of moisture, so they very rarely suffer from water shortage. However, the later sown ones can be spoiled if the ground becomes dry in the summer. Growth slows up and the skin hardens; then when

Carrots

93

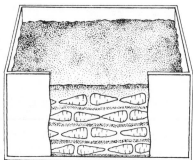
Storing carrots

if too small for that, put on the compost-heap), so that carrot rust flies are not attracted by the scent of exposed roots.

FERTILIZER   Since the continuous pulling of carrots takes a good deal out of the soil, and since the ground was not manured for this crop, it may be a good idea when the carrots are half-grown to give a light dressing of general fertilizer.

Lifting and storing

Carrots that have been left to grow to full size should be dug up at the end of the season before the first hard frosts of the winter, which may spoil them. Lift them carefully, using the fork, so as not to break them; if any do get damaged put them aside for immediate use, because they are likely to rot if you try to keep them. Remove the soil from the rest, cut off the leaves about an inch above the top of the root, and store them for winter use by laying them in a box, alternately head to tail, as shown, and covering each layer with sand or dry peat to stop them from shrivelling. If the box is put in a shed, garage, or other cool but frost-proof place, the roots should remain in good condition until the following spring.

Pests and diseases

Not many troubles afflict well-grown carrots, but the first one to be dealt with here can be extremely destructive.

CARROT RUST FLY   A close relation of the ordinary house-fly, this has a shiny green-black body, yellow head and legs. It appears in the spring and lays its eggs in the soil beside carrot plants, to which it is attracted by their smell. The eggs hatch in a few days, and the tiny grubs bite their way into the roots and feed almost without stopping on the sweet young carrot flesh for several days, becoming fat white maggots, as pictured here. The signs of their feasting are that the leaves droop in warm weather, turn a reddish color, then yellow, and finally wither and die. After two or three weeks the maggots pupate, to turn into flies, to lay more eggs, and so to ruin still more carrot crops.

By the time the maggots are fully fed the roots will be eaten away and most likely invaded by other

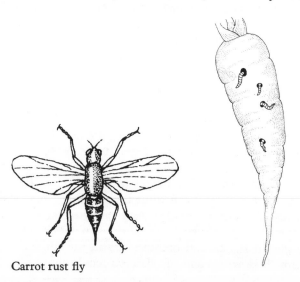
Carrot rust fly

creatures such as millipedes and wireworms, and it will be too late to do anything.

The time to start taking defensive action is before the flies lay their eggs. There are effective chemical pesticides sold for the purpose, and they can be sprinkled into the packet of seed as a protective dressing and the packet shaken until the seeds are covered with the powder. As an added precaution, the pesticide may also be sprinkled in the seed drill, as already explained under *Sowing*, where suggestions are also made for those who do not like using poisons.

VIOLET ROOT ROT   This fungus occasionally affects growing roots. It is not a serious disease, but infected plants should be removed before the infection spreads to healthy ones.

SCLEROTINIA ROT   This disease can be very serious indeed. It never attacks carrots during the growing season but it can turn stored roots into a useless mush covered with a woolly or fluffy fungus, as

Sclerotinia rot

pictured here. Nothing can be done to save infected roots by the time the disease is noticed; they must be taken away and burned before the fungus has time to infect the others, which it can do very quickly. To guard against the disease it is important to include only healthy roots in the store to begin with, and to examine the carrots every few weeks so that any doubtful looking ones may be removed.

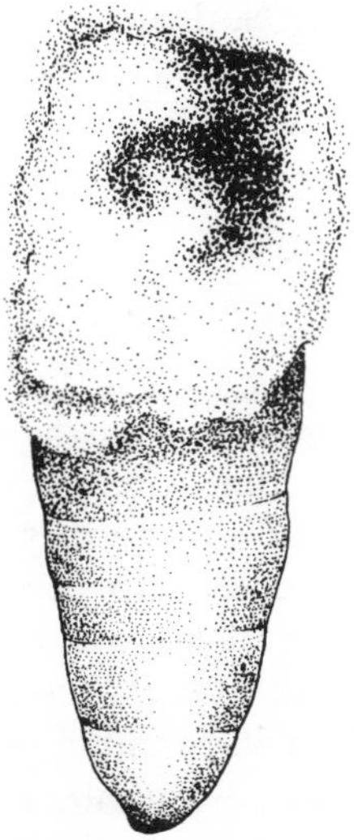

PARSNIPS
Some people find parsnips too coarse for their taste, and say they are fit only to feed cattle. Others think them to be one of the most delicious root vegetables, especially in the last few weeks of winter, when the frosts have made them sweet by turning much of the starch in them into sugar. Besides, if you find you have too many parsnips for eating, you can turn them into excellent wine.

Soil and manuring
Parsnips will grow in almost any soil so long as it is

Amount of seed required
$\frac{1}{4}$ oz. (c. 7 g.) will sow 30 ft. (c. 9 m.).

When to sow
Late winter to early spring, or during the fall where summers are hot.

Depth of drill
1 in. (c. 2.5 cm.).

Distance between rows
18 in. (c. 45 cm.).

Distance apart of plants
9 in. (c. 23 cm.).

Seedlings appear
In 3–4 weeks.

Ready to use
Mid fall to mid spring.

deep enough for them. Avoid freshly manured ground and prepare it for sowing in exactly the same way as for *carrots*.

Sowing

Parsnips do best if allowed a long period of growth. The seeds do not germinate easily and it may be several weeks before any seedlings appear. For that reason they should be sown as soon as you can get a good fine sowing surface on the ground; if that can be managed in late winter so much the better, but if the soil is still wet and sticky then wait until early spring when it is in better condition.

Draw a sowing drill 1 inch deep. Avoid sowing parsnip seeds on a windy day, because they are very light and can easily be blown away. Quite a high proportion of seeds in a packet are infertile and will never germinate, so parsnips are sown more thickly than carrots. Many people prefer not to sow the seeds all along the drill, but to place them in groups of three or four at intervals of 9 inches; when the seedlings come up, they can be thinned to leave only one at each place. Since parsnips are closely related to carrots they too are sometimes attacked by the carrot rust fly, so if this pest is troublesome on your vegetable plot you can guard against it in the same way as described under *Carrots*.

Care during growth

It is particularly important to get rid of weeds as soon as they appear. The reason is that parsnip seed can take a month or more to start into growth, and the seedlings will not have a proper chance if in the meantime the ground has become infested with weeds.

THINNING Do this as soon as the seedlings are big enough to handle, so that the ones left will have the longest possible time to grow without competition. Remove the thinnings and make the ground firm afterwards.

Pests and diseases

Parsnips are fairly trouble-free as a rule, but a few things sometimes attack them.

CARROT RUST FLY See *Carrots*.

WIREWORMS See *Garden foes*.

CANKER This disease is the most widespread and damaging trouble of parsnips. The symptoms are rust-colored patches, usually at the shoulder of the root, as shown. Sometimes they are darker and may even turn black, in which case they may eat deeply into the flesh and cause it to become putrid and slimy. Badly affected roots should be dug up and removed; often when the cankered top part has been cut off the rest will be found perfectly eatable. The disease can, however, usually be controlled by

Parsnips

Canker

spraying with Bordeaux mixture or Zineb.

There is evidence that canker, of all kinds, is worst where the parsnips are grown in heavy, wet ground. So make sure that the soil in which you sow them has been thoroughly cultivated and is well drained. It should also have sufficient lime. Some varieties of parsnip also seem much more susceptible to canker than others. The huge old fashioned kinds that still carry off prizes for length at vegetable shows, even though they are so hard and coarse as to be practically uneatable, usually have a sunken neck where the leaves join the root, and this sunken place holds the water when it rains and so is more likely to be infected by rot. So one way to reduce the risk of canker is to grow the smaller and more modern varieties of parsnip, which are much nicer to eat anyway.

TURNIPS

This vegetable might have appeared in this book in the section on *The cabbage family*, since it is a member of that group. As it is grown for its root,

however, it is more appropriately dealt with in this section. There are different varieties of turnip, ranging from the small, round, white ones which are very mild in flavor to the long, golden, red and purple topped ones with a much stronger taste.

Soil and manuring
Turnips will grow on almost any reasonable soil, but like all the other root vegetables, should not be grown in freshly manured ground. See that the soil contains enough lime, otherwise—as with all members of the cabbage family—there is a danger of club-root disease. A surface dressing of a complete fertilizer raked in before sowing will speed up growth.

Sowing
As turnips are very quick growing, they are usually grown either as an early crop on a piece of ground that will then be used for a later crop or as a quick 'catch-crop' between other vegetables that will not have grown big enough to need their full space until after the turnips have been gathered. Several

Turnips

small sowings of early and main crop kinds may be made from early spring to early summer, to provide young turnips in succession through the summer and fall. Turnips for use during the winter should not be sown before mid summer; if the ground is not ready for them by then, sowing can be delayed until late summer. Some gardeners sow what is left in the seed-packet in early fall, not to make roots but to provide young leaves for use as spring greens early the following year.

Care during growth
Keep the ground weeded from the moment the seedlings appear.

THINNING As soon as the young plants are an inch or two high they should be thinned. Give plenty of room for the roots to develop: 6 inches between the small early ones, 9–12 inches for main

---

Amount of seed required
¼ oz. (c. 7 g.) will sow 30 ft. (c. 9 m.).

When to sow
Early crop, early to mid spring. Winter crop, mid to late summer. For green leaves in spring, early fall.

Depth of drill
½ in. (c. 1 cm.).

Distance between rows
Early and Main crop, 12 in. (c. 30 cm.). Winter crop, 15 in. (c. 38 cm.).

Distance apart of plants
Early crop, 6 in. (c. 15 cm.). Main crop, 9 in. (c. 23 cm.). Winter crop, 12 in. (c. 30 cm.).

Seedlings appear
In about 7 days.

Ready to gather
In 8–12 weeks from sowing.

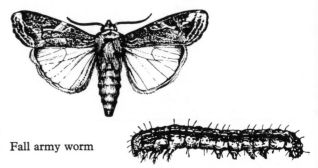

Fall army worm

crop and winter kinds. Do *not* thin the fall sown ones intended to produce spring greens. The more crowded they are, the more leaves they will form instead of roots.

Pests and diseases
Generally the same as for *Cabbages*, especially the destructive *Club-root* disease; this attacks white-fleshed turnips much more than it does the yellow-fleshed kinds.

FLEA-BEETLES can damage the young seedlings. See under *Radishes*.

CUTWORMS or surface caterpillars, of the Turnip Moth and the Fall army worm, pictured here, may spoil or even kill the plants by eating through them just below ground level. Deal with them as explained under *Lettuce*.

TURNIP SAWFLY This creature is one of a very large group of pests whose grubs make a nuisance of themselves in every part of the garden, from the ones that roll the leaves of roses to those that wriggle about inside infected apples. The grubs have a tremendous appetite and can nibble young plants down to worthless stumps. If tackled soon enough they can be controlled by a suitable pesticide,

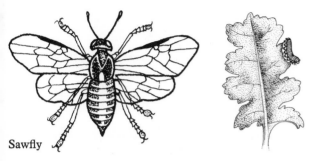

Sawfly

or simply squashed between thumb and finger.

SOFT ROT This does not usually attack except through a wound, such as a crack in the skin caused by irregular growth caused by dry weather. When it does occur it can, as shown, reduce the inside of the root to a soft putrid mass. Remove all infected roots at once.

Gathering the crop

Summer and autumn turnips are pulled and eaten as required. Winter ones may be left in the ground until the spring. If you fear very severe frost, however, they may be lifted and stored like *Carrots*.

Soft rot

RUTABAGA

These useful vegetables are a kind of milder, sweeter and hardier turnip. Since they grow much more slowly they should be sown in late spring, and will then be ready to eat by winter. In all respects they are treated like *Turnips*, and suffer the same troubles (though usually not so badly).

KOHLRABI

The name means 'Cabbage-turnip', and the part that is eaten is really the swollen stem, not the root. It is sown any time from early spring to early summer, in the fall in mild winter areas, and treated in exactly the same way as *Turnips*.

Kohlrabi

Twisting off leaves

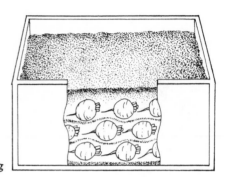

Storing

BEET

An easy vegetable to grow, beet takes up little space and if sown in small amounts several times can be pulled during the summer and fall.

Soil, manuring, sowing, thinning
Same as for *Carrots*.

Amount of seed required
¼ oz. (c. 7 g.) will sow 40 ft. (c. 12 m.).

When to sow
Mid spring to early summer, earlier in hot summer regions.

Depth of drill
1 in. (c. 2.5 cm.).

Distance between rows
12 in. (c. 30 cm.).

Distance apart of plants
4–5 in. (c. 10–12 cm.).

Seedlings appear
In about 8 days.

Ready to gather
Early summer to mid fall from open. Lift roots for storing before frost.

Lifting
Pull the roots while they are still young and tender; if left too long they go woody. It is believed by many that beet will bleed and lose color if the leaves are cut off, so they are twisted off, as shown.

Storing
Carefully lift all roots before frosts start. Remove any damaged ones. The rest can be stored in boxes, covered with sand or peat in a frost-proof place.

Beetroot

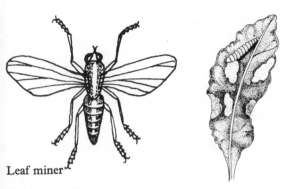

Leaf miner

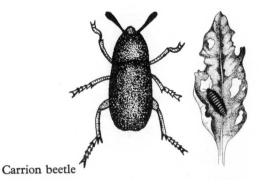

Carrion beetle

Pests and diseases

So long as the soil is kept reasonably moist, so that the roots do not become hard and cracked, very few troubles normally occur.

LEAF MINER, shown here, can be a nuisance. The maggots bore into the leaves, making blisters and causing them to shrivel. Affected leaves should be picked off and crushed, or a suitable insecticide used.

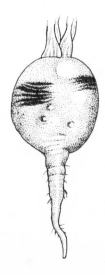

Beet rust

THE CARRION BEETLE is a close relation of the beetles that live on the decaying bodies of dead animals, but is wholly vegetarian. Pictured here, it lives in the soil and lays its eggs there. When the young hatch out they climb the plants and chew the young leaves. They may be dealt with in the same way as the maggots of the *Leaf miner* (see above).

BEET RUST can, as illustrated, disfigure beet by the invasion of a fungus that causes dark brown, spreading spots. Little can be done except to burn infected plants and to make sure you never grow beets in the same ground two years running.

SALSIFY

This delicious vegetable is sometimes called the 'vegetable oyster' because of its flavor. Though a member of the daisy family, and so no relation, it has roots that look rather like thin parsnips. It should be sown in early to mid spring and treated exactly like *Parsnips*.

SCORZONERA

This vegetable is very like a black-skinned kind of salsify, and is treated in the same way. If grown between rows of carrots, scorzonera is said by some people to drive away the destructive carrot rust fly.

23. Celery

THERE ARE two quite different sorts of celery: the green kind, which takes a good deal of hard work, will stand quite severe frost and tastes superb, and the summer—or 'self-blanching' or golden kind, which takes much less effort, will not stand frost at all and tastes at best quite good and at worst nasty. Since the two sorts need quite different treatment, they are dealt with separately here.

GREEN CELERY

There are several varieties available from seedsmen, ranging in color from snow-white, through rose-pink, to ruby-red. The white looks and tastes best but is the least hardy.

Sowing

Winter celery needs a long season of growth, so it should be sown early, under glass. If you have a greenhouse or a small propagator, sow in a seed-tray filled with soil (or better still a seed mix, which can be bought ready prepared) by scattering the seed thinly on the surface and covering lightly with sand or fine soil. Water thoroughly and stand the tray, covered with glass, in a temperature of 65–70°F. A window-sill in a warm room will do if you have no other facilities. When the seedlings appear, thin them to an inch or two apart and put the tray in a somewhat cooler place to harden them off.

If you prefer, you can buy excellent plants from a nursery when planting time comes. These will save you a good deal of bother and will probably be better than anything you can raise yourself anyway.

Soil and manuring

Celery needs a good deal of ground if it is to be grown properly. If you have not much space to spare, you can wait until a patch has been cleared of an early crop, such as peas, so long as the planting is done before mid summer and the seedlings are not allowed to get overcrowded.

TRENCHES To get really good sticks, you should grow celery in trenches excavated to the full depth of your spade. Make the trench 12 inches wide for a single row, or 18 inches wide for a double row. Break up the bottom soil and spread over it a good layer of organic, moisture-holding material such as well-rotted manure or compost. In its natural surroundings, celery always grows beside rivers and ponds, so the soil can hardly be too moist for it.

Tread the layer of organic material well down and then cover it with some of the excavated topsoil until the level of the trench comes about 4 inches lower than the surface of the ground. The remainder of the excavated topsoil should be neatly mounded into a ridge on each side of the trench (far enough

---

Amount of seed required
A small packet will give hundreds of plants.

When to sow
Early to mid spring. Or grow as a winter crop in the south.

Depth to sow
Cover seed lightly.

Seedlings appear
Within about 3 weeks.

When to plant out
Early to mid summer.

Width of trench
Single rows, 12 in. (c. 30 cm.).
Double rows, 18 in. (c. 45 cm.).

Distance apart of plants
9 in (c. 23 cm.).

Ready to use
Late fall onwards.

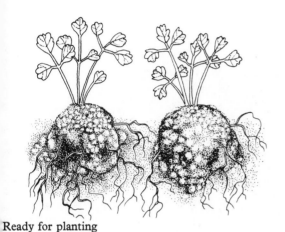

Ready for planting

from the edge not to fall in) and may be used to grow quick-maturing salad crops, such as lettuces and radish, which will have been removed and eaten before the ridged soil is needed for earthing up the celery.

Now tread down the replaced soil in the trench until it is really firm, by which time it will be about 6 inches below ground-level. Rake in a good dressing of a general fertilizer and the trench is ready for planting.

Planting out

During early to mid summer, the celery seedlings should be transplanted into the prepared trench. Water the box of young plants thoroughly and leave it to drain for an hour before transplanting, so that the roots are damaged as little as possible.

Take out planting-holes with a trowel, 9 inches apart, either in a single line along the center of the 12-inch wide trench or in a zigzag double line along each side of the 18-inch trench; the double row is a saving of space and labor because you get twice the number of plants for very little extra effort or space. If any of the plants have side-shoots (called

'suckers') growing from the base, remove such side-shoots, as shown here, before planting. If left, they will spoil the growth of the plant and make earthing-up impossible.

Spread the roots of the seedlings out carefully, cover them with soil and tread firmly; they should be anchored so well that if you try to pull them out by a leaf, the leaf tears first. Then water the plants well in.

Care during growth

If the sun is hot, the newly planted seedlings may need watering again during the next week or so, to prevent them from shrivelling while the roots repair themselves and start growing again.

When the plants recover from the operation and start growing rapidly, they will benefit from being fed with liquid fertilizer, which can be bought from any garden supplier and is diluted with water before use; ask for a vegetable grade, which has a different balance of ingredients from those sold for use on flowers.

EARTHING UP When the plants are about 12 inches high the stems should be drawn together and tied (loosely, to allow for further growth) with raffia or

Removing sideshoots

Celery

soft string. The first earthing up may now be given. First remove any more side-shoots growing from the base of the plants, then shovel earth from the ridges down into the trench until it comes about a quarter of the way up the stalks. In two or three weeks a second lot of earth should be shovelled around the plants, bringing it halfway up the stems, which will make it level with, or slightly above, the surface of the ground.

One or two more earthings-up will bring the ridge of soil nearly up to the green leaves and well above ground level. Make the sides of the ridge sloping, as pictured, so that rain runs off instead of into the center of the plants. Do not earth up too high. The green leaves should be well above the soil or the plants will be smothered.

Some people wrap the stalks with cardboard collars or sleeves, or even newspaper, before earthing, because they say it keeps the hearts of the plants cleaner and deters slugs. Some gardeners only use the collars for blanching, while others say such wrappings encourage slugs, earwigs, and all

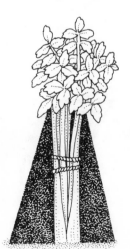

Earthing up

kinds of pests by providing them with a cosy home. Try each method and see which gives the best result for you.

Digging
Celery will be ready by late fall, but many people say it becomes better if left longer, because a few hard frosts make it sweeter and crisper. Since you leave celery in the ground and dig it only as you want it, you will be able to decide for yourself whether you think it improves or not.

Never try to *pull* up celery. If it is as crisp as it should be, it will only break off and be spoiled. Dig the fork in carefully (from well to the side, so as not to spear the plant) until it is right under the base, and then lever the plant gently out of the ground. Cut off the top leaves and the roots, and put them on the compost heap, together with any damaged outer stalks, which should be pulled off at the base.

SELF-BLANCHING CELERY
This name is really quite inaccurate. It was probably thought up by a publicity man to suggest that this type of celery is just the same as the green kind but somehow magically blanches itself without needing all the hard work involved in the tedious earthing-up that ordinary celery demands.

In fact, it is quite a different type, which just happens to have stems that are creamy yellow (or 'golden', as the seedsmen call them) because they are deficient in chlorophyll and so cannot turn green. (To confuse matters, there is now also a green-stemmed variety called 'green self-blanching', which seems a contradiction in terms.)

So long as the difference is recognized, self-blanching celery can be very good to eat in the late summer and early fall, though it is never quite as nice as ordinary celery (nor as nasty, one must add,

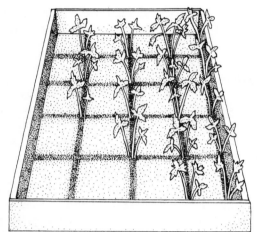

Planting in a frame

Green Celery (see above). If you have no facilities t[o] raise plants from seed, you can buy them from [a] nursery.

Soil and manuring

Being quicker-growing than the green kind, self[-] blanching celery needs a good rich soil with plent[y] of nourishment. Though it will produce quite goo[d] crops in the open ground, it will do much better i[f] the plants are grown in a frame—not anythin[g] elaborate with glass over it, but just four board[s] 9 inches or so wide, set on edge in an oblong an[d] either joined together at the corners or simply hel[d] in place with pegs driven into the ground. Rak[e] some general fertilizer into the soil, then set th[e] first row of plants, 9 inches apart, against the boar[d] along one side, then another row 9 inches from that[,] as shown, and so on until the frame is completel[y] filled with plants 9 inches apart from each other eac[h] way. This close planting will really keep the celer[y] blanched as it grows.

Planting

This should be done with a trowel, side-shoots bein[g] first removed from the base of the plants as explaine[d]

because it is all gone by the time that snow, ice, slugs and decay have made a hollow mockery of ordinary celery).

Because self-blanching celery is much quicker-growing than the green kind, it should never be sown before mid spring. If you sow it earlier, in the hope of getting an extra-early crop, just one or two late frosts will make it run to seed. In all other respects, sowing is exactly the same as for

Celery looper

Celery worm

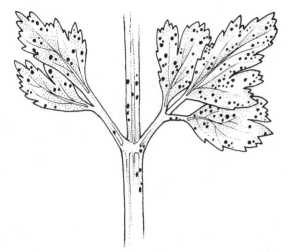

Late blight

Black heart

for *Green Celery*. Water the plants well in.

Digging
Self-blanching celery will be ready to eat during early to mid fall. Lift it with the fork, as explained for *Winter Celery*. Finish lifting before the frosts start; it cannot survive freezing.

Pests and diseases
The same troubles attack both kinds of celery, so they are all dealt with together here.

SLUGS   See under *Garden foes*.

CELERY LOOPER   Found throughout the country and similar in appearance to the cabbage looper. Rotenone is effective against them.

CELERY WORM   The larva of the black swallowtail butterfly, as pictured here, which damages the plant by chewing the leaves. An effective remedy is to

spray with rotenone or pyrethrum.

LATE BLIGHT   This is far the most serious disease of celery. It causes brown spotting on the foliage and stems, as shown, and in bad cases can completely cripple the plants. Late blight is caused by infected seed, and will not occur if the seed has been treated with a disinfectant against it. Most seed sold by reputable nurseries nowadays has been treated in this way, which makes it poisonous to the disease germs (and to human beings, so wash your hands after touching it).

BLACK HEART   This is caused by a microscopic organism which turns the heart of the plant into a slimy, rotten mass. Affected plants should be removed at once before the disease spreads. Infection is through wounds caused by slugs and other gnawing creatures, or even by very hard frost. So keep slugs at bay as far as possible, and protect the plants with straw or bracken in severe weather.

24. Salads

IT SHOULD BE possible, with a little planning, for all vegetable growers to enjoy fresh salads every day even if your winters are cold.

If you have a greenhouse, that should not be too difficult, even during the winter; but even if you have not, a cold frame or a row or two of cloches made of glass or plastic should enable you to achieve the ideal of something fresh every day, or try growing one or two extra-hardy things in the open. You can even produce tasty cress on a window-sill in your home. Perhaps you think salads are too cold for eating in the winter? You may be right. But it is largely a matter of habit; once you have got the taste for something fresh every day you will wonder how you could ever have enjoyed life without it. Your health should improve too.

LETTUCES
Though all the lettuces we eat are descended from the same wild species, *Lactuca sativa*, they have over many years been developed by plant breeders into separate types so unlike each other that you might think they were entirely different.

There are basically four types of cultivated lettuce, each excellent for different purposes and each available in several varieties. The romaine or cos lettuce, with tall, pointed leaves, is generally considered to be the best in flavor and is crunchy to eat; but it breaks rather easily and it cannot stand dry weather, which turns it tough. Then there are two head lettuce types (listed by some seedsmen as 'cabbage lettuces', though they are no relations of the cabbage). One is the crisphead kind, which is at its best in the summer—solid-hearted, able to stand up to drought, and so crisp that you can hardly handle the leaves without breaking them. The other is the butterhead or bibb kind, which is generally hardier and so does better in cold weather;

Amount of seed required
¼ oz. (c. 7 g.) will sow 50 ft. (c. 15 m.).

When to sow
Summer crop, early spring to mid summer. Spring crop, late summer Extra-early crop, fall to winter.

Depth of drill
½ in. (c. 1 cm.).

Distance between rows
12 in. (c. 30 cm.).

Distance apart of plants
Small kinds, 9 in. (c. 23 cm.). Large kinds, 12 in. (c. 30 cm.).

Seedlings appear
Within a week.

Full-sized
In 2–3 months.

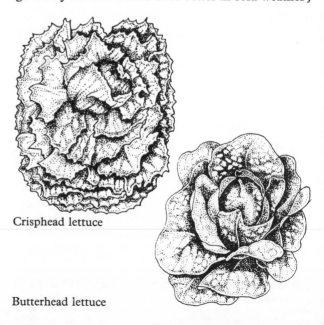

Crisphead lettuce

Butterhead lettuce

Cos or romaine lettuce

it is sold in far greater numbers than the others and storekeepers say it is more popular, but perhaps they mean it is more popular with them rather than their customers, because it is not so easily bruised owing to its softer leaves (which some customers have been heard to call flabby).

The fourth type, the loose-leaf lettuce, is completely different in appearance from the other three. It was developed under such names as 'Salad Bowl' and does not have a heart at all but is open-centered and consists of a large number of loosely arranged leaves; this type has none of the crispness associated with ordinary lettuce, but is said by health-food fanciers to be much better for you because it has far more chlorophyll and is nearer to the original wild lettuce.

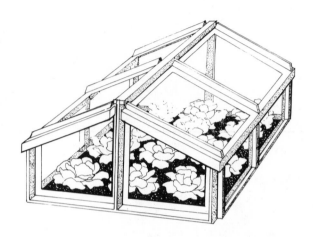

Soil and manuring

Lettuces do best in rich soil containing plenty of organic matter, such as manure or compost. They will not grow well in acid conditions, so make sure the soil has enough lime.

Since lettuces grow quickly and so do not occupy the ground for long, they are not usually grown on their own but in odd places that would otherwise be left unused for a short time, such as the ground between rows of slower-growing vegetables that will not take up their full space for two or three months, by which time the lettuces will have been used. Since lettuces demand moist soil, they will benefit from the shade of the other crops.

Lettuce may also be sown between rows of quick-growing vegetables (early peas for instance) a few weeks before they are harvested; in this case it will be the other crop that is removed first, leaving space for the lettuce to develop.

A very good place for a quick crop of summer lettuce is the ridges of soil alongside celery trenches before that soil is needed for earthing-up. A good deal of watering may be required here, because the ridges, being above ground level, will tend to dry out.

Sowing

Rake a sprinkling of general fertilizer into the surface of the soil, and then draw the sowing drill $\frac{1}{2}$ inch deep. Sow the lettuce thinly along this (the seed is very light, so be careful the wind does not snatch it away), cover the soil again, tread it down firmly and rake lightly. If the weather is dry, finish with a good watering.

If the ground is in a suitable condition, the first sowing of lettuce may be made in late winter, but this early sowing may need protection in colder parts of the country. Cover them either by plastic caps or cloches made from glass, fiberglass or plastic or raise them in a cold frame. Such cloches are a very good investment, since they can also be used to protect later-sown lettuces for use in late fall and early winter. Choose a small, butterhead variety for this early sowing; your local nurseryman will advise you on a suitable kind for your area of the country.

The first unprotected outdoor sowing in areas

other than the south and southwest may be made in early spring. From then until mid summer, make a small sowing every two or three weeks, to give you a regular supply of fresh lettuce right through the summer and into the late fall.

The secret of success with lettuce is to sow *little* and *often*. Then you will not only get a succession throughout the season but will avoid waste; lettuce does not stand still for long, and if you cannot use it soon after it has reached maturity, it will quickly run to seed and become bitter and unusable.

There are many different varieties suitable for these spring and summer sowings. Ask your nurseryman about them. Study the pictures on the packets; they may seem too good to be true, but they will show you what the different types look like. Grow several different kinds, to add the spice of variety to your salads throughout the season. Include at least one variety of cos lettuce; to make sure that it produces crisp, white hearts the plants may be tied loosely round with raffia or soft string, as pictured, before they are full grown.

The last outdoor sowings are made in late summer, and may be of two kinds. If you have cloches, you can sow one of the hardier varieties in mid summer; leave the plants unprotected until early fall, when you can cover them with cloches and look forward to having salads from them in late fall and early winter. The second summer sowing is later in the season. For this, use the hardiest kinds specially bred to stand without protection through the harshest winter weather. They include head and cos varieties and often have words like 'Arctic' and 'winter' in their names, though they do not produce hearts until the following spring.

Care during growth

Remove weeds as soon as they appear. If slugs are around, scatter slug bait along the row to stop the seedlings being eaten as they come up.

THINNING   Lettuce seedlings very quickly become drawn and floppy if they are allowed to remain overcrowded for a few days. Since even the thinnest of sowings are bound to be a little uneven in places, pull out any overcrowded seedlings as soon as you can handle them. Do not try to transplant these thinnings; they will amost certainly run to seed.

Repeat the thinning operation several times over the next few weeks until the remaining plants are at their final distance apart—from 9 inches for the small varieties to 12 inches for the large ones.

Do not thin the hardy kinds sown in late summer until the spring; let them huddle together for warmth during the winter.

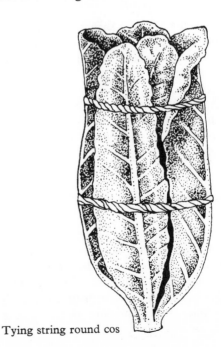

Tying string round cos

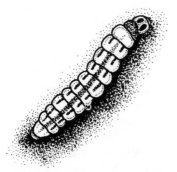

Cutworm

Pests and diseases

Unfortunately lettuce is attacked by a number of things, of which the worst are listed below.

SLUGS AND SNAILS See *Garden foes*.

CUTWORMS When you find a thriving lettuce plant suddenly flop, and discover that the stem has been bitten through at soil level, the culprit is almost certainly a cutworm, or surface caterpillar, like the one shown here.

There are many different kinds. They usually eat at night and hide under stones or clods of earth by day. Seek them out and destroy them. If your ground is badly infested, you can apply a suitable pesticide powder to the soil.

APHIDS See *Garden foes*.

DOWNY MILDEW This disease shows its presence by a furry coating under the leaves and yellow patches on top, as illustrated. It can be serious under glass but is sometimes a nuisance in the open. Suitable sprays can help, but the disease is mainly caused by humid conditions and overcrowding. Thin seedlings early to prevent this.

GRAY MOLD Infection by *Botrytis cinerea*—a common scourge of nearly all plant life—causes this disease, which, as shown, covers the plant with a gray, velvet-like coating. It causes rotting at ground level, in bad cases parting the top growth completely from the roots so that it collapses. The infection is thought to enter the plant at ground level, only through damaged tissue, such as dead leaves. Remove badly affected plants before the infection spreads. Fungicide sprays can guard against it, but the avoidance of damage and overcrowding are the most important means of prevention.

TIP BURN As pictured here, and as suggested by the name, this causes dead, brown patches at the tips of leaves. It is worst under glass, but sometimes

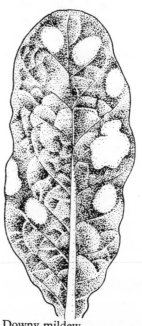

Downy mildew

Gray mold

Tip burn

damages plants in the open. It is not a disease, but scorching thought to be caused by hot sun and dryness at the roots. The remedy is to grow lettuce in moist soil with plenty of organic matter in it and to water the plants if necessary.

ENDIVE AND CHICORY

This green salad crop has been developed by plant-breeders from the beautiful blue-flowered wild plant called chicory (*Cichorium endivia*) and is extremely hardy, giving fresh leaves in the bitterest winter weather. There are two kinds offered by seedsmen: the curled-leaved and the broad-leaved (sometimes called escargle or Batavian). The curled-leaved is usually sown in early to mid summer for late fall use, and the broad-leaved in late summer for winter use. Treat both kinds exactly like lettuces, and give no protection at all. The plants can, however, be covered with large flower-pots, placed upside down, a few weeks before cutting them to blanch them and make them sweeter. A more modern strain has now come on the market called 'Sugarhat Chicory', which is self-blanching, looks rather like a large cos

Endive

Growing mustard and cress

lettuce, and can be sown in mid summer to mature in late fall. This strain forms crisp, solid hearts and remains in good condition in the open ground for months.

Another type of chicory, called Witloof or French Chicory, is sown in late spring and produces roots rather like parsnips. These roots are lifted in late fall, the tops having been cut off an inch or two

above the crown (do not slice the root itself) and stored in boxes in a cool, but frost-proof, place. Plant the roots in a batch of five or six in a large flowerpot full of peat, place another flowerpot upside down over it to keep out the light, bring it into a warm place (not too hot—the average kitchen temperature will do) and in a few weeks you will be able to cut delicious forced shoots, or 'chicons', for

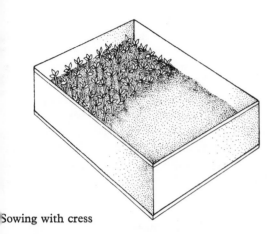

Sowing with cress

winter salads. Successive batches of roots, forced in the same way, will give you fresh chicons throughout the winter.

MUSTARD AND CRESS

These are the easiest of all green salad plants to grow, and do not need a garden. Put some damp peat in a small container, press it down, sprinkle seed thickly on the surface, cover with plastic film and stand it on the kitchen window sill. When the seed germinates you can remove the covering, and as soon as the green tops have grown high enough cut off the young plants with scissors. If you want to eat mustard and cress together, sow one half of the container with cress and wait for four days before sowing the other half with mustard, which is quicker to germinate.

RADISHES

These are the quickest to mature of all salad vegetables, and if sown little and often will provide a crop over a very long season.

Soil and manuring

Radishes are not particular about soil. In any case,

ground is hardly ever prepared specially for them because they are usually grown as a quick 'catch-crop' between rows of other vegetables or on odd bits of land that happen to be vacant for a month or two. The radishes will have matured, been pulled up and eaten within a few weeks.

Sowing

The first sowing may be made in early spring (or even late winter in warm places). Draw shallow drills, and sow the seed *thinly* along them. Continue to sow short rows every two or three weeks throughout the season until the early fall.

Care during growth

Radishes need very little attention indeed, beyond the removal of weeds and precautions against flea-beetle (dealt with later, under *Pests*).

THINNING should not be necessary if the sowing was not done too thickly. All the seedlings should be allowed to reach usable size.

Amount of seed required
¼ oz. (c. 7 g.). will sow 50 ft. (c. 15m.).

When to sow
Early spring to early fall.

Depth of Drill
½ in. (c. 1 cm.).

Distance between rows
6 in. (c. 15 cm.).

Seedlings appear
Within a week.

Full sized
In 5–6 weeks.

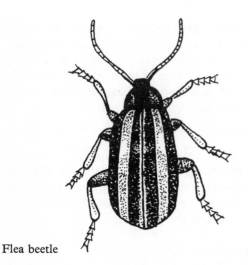

Flea beetle

turnips, but is particularly destructive to radishes. It is a tiny black creature that attacks the seedlings as soon as they germinate, riddling the seed-leaves with holes and, if not checked, so weakening the plants that they give a miserable crop, or even die. The most effective way to protect the crop at present is to dust the seed immediately after sowing with a suitable insecticide powder, dust again after covering the drill in, and at the first sign of an attack dust the seedlings. Keep the plants growing vigorously; as they get bigger they become less vulnerable to this pest.

SCAB   This trouble is caused by the same fungus that causes potato scab. It shows as brown sunken places, as pictured here, and can make affected radishes inedible—or at least unpalatable. Scab is worst in poor, dry ground; so grow radishes in fairly rich, moist soil.

Pulling

Pull the radishes for use as soon as they are big enough. Go along the whole row pulling the largest ones so that those left can develop and be pulled in their turn. Do not leave any to become coarse and woody.

Winter radishes

These are quite different from the summer kind, growing much bigger (up to 1 lb.) and having either black, white or rose-pink skin over white flesh, which can be shredded to make crisp winter salads. Sow in mid summer in rows 12 inches apart and thin the plants to 9 inches apart.

Pests and diseases

Being a member of the same group, the radish may suffer from any of the same troubles as those dealt with in the section *The cabbage family*.

FLEA BEETLE   This pest, pictured here, also attacks other members of the cabbage family, including

Radish scab

Radishes

25. Tomatoes and their relatives

THE TOMATO has become such an important part of our diet, and such a vital ingredient in what we think of as our traditional dishes, that it is quite difficult to realize that less than four centuries ago it was unknown except to remote tribes in parts of tropical South America, where it was discovered growing wild. Its cousin the pepper (with the hot-flavored variety called the chili) was also found in the tropical zone of America, but somewhat later; the natives had cultivated it over the ages, but nobody is now able to find where it originated in the wild.

Another cousin, the eggplant, so called because there used to be a white, egg-shaped variety—is also a native of the tropics, though in this case the tropics of Africa and Asia.

It stands to reason, then, that, since the tomato, the pepper and the eggplant are all tropical plants, the most satisfactory way to grow them in cooler regions is in greenhouses. This book, however, is not written for those with greenhouses, so we will only concern ourselves with how to grow these plants in the open.

TOMATOES

Through very skillful breeding and selection, the modern cultivated tomato has been developed along two different lines, resulting in two very distinct types of plant. The first, usually called the standard, or indeterminate—that is, it keeps on growing upwards until it gets so long that it has to be stopped by the grower. It is usually pruned to a single or double main stem, from which all the leaves and bunches of fruit grow. All the greenhouse varieties and many of the outdoor ones are of this type, and because of their lengthwise habit of growth they have to be artificially supported.

Single stem indeterminate tomato

Bush or determinate tomato

The second kind of tomato is called the 'bush' or determinate type. It is determinate in growth—that is, when it has reached a certain height it stops. After that, it does not get any taller, but grows sideways, sending out plenty of new shoots and becoming wide-spreading and bushy, as pictured here. It tends to get untidy in habit, and because of the space it takes up it is only really suitable for growing in the open. It is (theoretically at least) self-supporting and does not need training.

Varieties

There are several different varieties of each of the two types. Since growing conditions and temperatures vary from district to district, it is a good idea to ask your local nurseryman for varieties most likely to succeed in your area; he should know what grows and crops best for his customers. You can

Amount of seed required
A small packet will give plenty of plants.

When to sow
Early to mid spring, under glass, in heat unless the weather is mild.

How to sow
In pots or boxes of seed starting mix.

Seedlings appear
In 8–10 days.

When to plant out
Late spring to early summer.

Distance between rows
2 ft. 6 in. (c. 75 cm.).

Distance apart of plants
18 in. (c. 45 cm.).

buy tomato plants at the appropriate time ready to plant out, or you can raise your own from seed.

Sowing

To germinate and grow properly in their early stages, tomatoes must have a minimum temperature of 60°F (15°C). A minimum of 65°F (18°C) is better. That means you must have a heated greenhouse or helpful neighbors or friends who can spare you a space in theirs. A sunny window sill in your kitchen or living room can be used for growing plants of a sort, but since the light will be coming from one side, they will tend to be curved and weak unless boosted by artificial lighting.

Take a seed flat (a discarded plastic container will do, but make holes in the bottom for water to drain away) and put seed mix into it until it is three-quarters full. Seed mix can be bought in small amounts from most garden suppliers. Press down the surface of the compost so that it is level and sow the seeds on this an inch apart. Cover the seed with more compost just enough to hide it and finish by watering. As soon as the seedlings have made their first pair of leaves, transplant them into 3-inch pots of potting soil; be very careful not to damage the roots during this operation. After that water the plants as necessary (but not too much, because they hate wet roots) and harden them off by moving them into a lower temperature (about 55°F is ideal). On warm days they can be stood outside, or the windows or ventilators opened wide, so that it will not come as too much of a shock to them when they are planted out.

Don't sow your tomatoes too early even though they are protected from the outdoor weather or they will be too big, and too set in their indoor habits, when planting-out time comes.

If you have no facilities for raising plants from seed, or you simply do not want to be bothered, you can buy plants from any good nursery. They are likely to be better than anything you can raise yourself anyway.

Soil and manuring

When picking-time comes you will have to tread many times on both sides of the row of plants to do the gathering. It is wise, therefore, to grow your tomatoes in such a place that you do not keep trampling on other crops while you are picking. A position by a path at the end of your vegetable plot would be ideal.

Well grown tomato plants yield an amazing amount of fruit, so they have to be fed very well to replace all the goodness they are taking from the earth. For that reason the soil in which they are planted should be as rich as you can possible make it. Plenty of well rotted manure or compost should have been dug in—preferably in the fall, but failing that several weeks before planting time. A good dressing of a general fertilizer raked into the ground a few days before planting will get the tomatoes off to a flying start; for super-special results use a special tomato fertilizer with a high potassium content. Avoid high-nitrogen fertilizers; they make leaves at the expense of fruit.

Planting out

This should not be done before all danger of frost is over—the time will obviously depend on your local weather conditions.

Do not try to beat the calendar by planting too

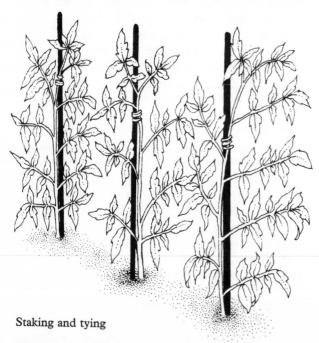

Staking and tying

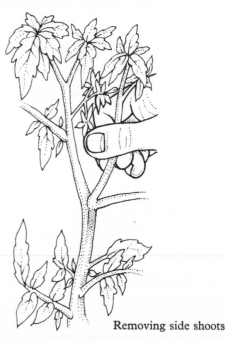

Removing side shoots

soon in the hope of getting earlier tomatoes. In fact you will only succeed in getting later ones, because once a tomato plant has been frosted it will take a long time to recover, and plants put in later which have not suffered from frost will grow quicker and crop sooner. A good tip is to watch when your neighboring amateur gardening experts plant out their tomatoes, and plant yours out a week later. If the experts really were experts you will have lost very little time; if not, it will be their plants that have suffered, not yours.

Before removing the young plants from their pots, give them a good watering; that will make it easier to knock them gently out of the pots without damaging the roots. Make planting holes with a trowel and, keeping the ball of soil round the roots intact, lower the plant into the hole so that the top of the ball of soil comes just below the surface. Then fill in the hole and tread firmly all round the plant. Finish with a good watering.

If you are growing single-stem, or 'cordon', tomatoes, push a stout stake about 5 feet long into the ground beside each plant for support. If you are growing the bush type of tomato, no support is needed.

Care during growth

In the early stages after transplanting, the most important thing is to see that the young plants do not suffer from lack of water; if they do, they will never fully recover. A good way to make sure the water gets to the roots is to make a hole with a trowel beside each plant and fill it up with the watering can. Some people sink a large flowerpot in each hole and fill that up.

TYING   As single stem plants grow taller, they need tying to their stakes for support. Do this quite

Mulching with straw

loosely, as shown, and continue until the plants reach the top of their stakes.

SIDE-SHOOT REMOVAL   This is a rather tedious and time-consuming operation, but it has to be done regularly, otherwise the plants will become unmanageable. Like tying, it is a job that is only needed with single stem plants. As shown in the illustration, side shoots appear at each junction of the main stem with a leaf. Every one of these side-shoots must be removed; just pinch it out between finger and thumb.

LEAF REMOVAL AND STOPPING   As the flowers appear and are followed by the formation of fruits, some lower leaves will begin to turn yellow. Remove them cleanly from the stem.

Tomatoes

FEEDING When the fruit is swelling, give the plants a feed of liquid fertilizer (buy the special tomato mixture) every week.

MULCHING If you are growing the bush type of tomato, which needs no support or side shoot removal, it is a good idea to lay straw under the plants, as shown on p. 121, to prevent fruit from touching the soil and being splashed with mud.

Picking
As the fruits ripen and become fully colored, gather them carefully. Put your thumb against the fruit-stalk, lift the fruit up in the palm of your hand, and it will come cleanly away.

The day after the first frosty night, pick all remaining fruits. Many of them will ripen on a window-sill or in a drawer; the rest can be used unripe to make green tomato chutney.

Pests and diseases
One trouble to watch out for, particularly in damp weather, is *Blight*. This is the same disease that attacks *Potatoes* and is treated in the same way.

BLOSSOM-END ROT Shown here is a typical example of this disorder, which withers the end of the fruit. It happens only to plants that have been dry at the roots; regular watering will prevent it.

MOTH Caterpillars of some moths can cause great damage by gnawing both leaves and ripening fruit, as pictured here. Seek them out and destroy them.

GRAY MOLD This very common fungus attacks damaged tissue, especially in damp, cold conditions. Remove cleanly all dead or decaying stumps of leaves and fallen fruit to stop the disease.

VIRUS There are many types of virus that affect tomatoes. That pictured here, called Common Mosaic, is the commonest and causes mottling and distortion of the leaves. Remove and destroy all virus-infected plants. There is no known cure.

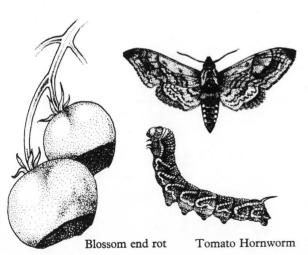

Blossom end rot   Tomato Hornworm   Gray mold   Common mosaic

PEPPERS

Plant breeders have developed garden varieties, which the amateur can grow, of both the mild-tasting sweet pepper and its pungent variety the chilli. They may be successfully treated in exactly the same way as the tomato, to which they are closely related.

EGGPLANTS

Plant breeders have been busy with the eggplant too, and have developed easy-to-grow garden varieties. The first-generation crosses called F1 hybrids are very reliable, producing good crops of excellent, smooth-skinned fruit. The eggplant is, however, the least hardy of the vegetables dealt with in this section, and can suffer badly from cold. Some people avoid the trouble by growing their plants in large pots, as shown, and bringing them indoors at night during a cold spell.

Eggplants

Eggplants in pot

Peppers

26. The cucumber family

OF ALL THE THINGS we grow in our vegetable gardens, the members of this family, the 'cucurbits' that includes cucumbers, pumpkins, melons and squashes, are perhaps most like their wild ancestors and least willing to be tamed. Coming as they do from steaming jungles in the hotter parts of the world, they grow faster than the rest of our crops and if they were not kept in order they would soon smother any other vegetables within their reach. They should not therefore be grown between rows of other crops, but need a patch to themselves. If you are not able to give them this, you will have to economize on space by growing them in the air, training the vines upward on fences or trellises or grow cucumbers in a wooden tub, barrel or large box.

There is another great problem with the cucumber family in these days of modern chemicals to control pests. All the members of the family are extremely sensitive to a great many of the most efficient pesticides on the market. So it is very important before spraying cucumbers and the like to make absolutely sure that the chemical will not harm them. An unsuitable product can kill them within a few hours.

That is another reason why the members of this group of plants should be grown on their own. Even if you take great care not to use the wrong product on them, a few drops of an unsuitable chemical drifting accidentally on to them during the spraying of a neighbouring crop could cause severe damage or even death.

Amount of seed required
A packet contains 5–20 seeds, according to variety.

When to sow
Mid spring under glass. Early summer outdoors.

Depth to sow
1 in. (c. 2.5 cm.).

When to plant
Early summer.

Distance between plants
30 in. (c. 75 cm.).

Seedlings appear
Within 7–10 days.

Ready to pick
Mid summer onwards.

CUCUMBERS
Varieties
Do not buy varieties that are described by seedsmen as being suitable both for indoor and for outdoor growing; that simply means that they are not much good for either.

Choose a kind that is sold only for outdoor growing. These days it does not have to be one of the old-fashioned, thick-skinned kinds covered with knobbly warts and having hard, leathery flesh which causes horrible indigestion. In the last few years some much more attractive kinds have been bred which not only have skin nearly as smooth as store-bought ones but are easy on the digestion. 'Burpless' is the name under which they are sold; the seed is a good deal more expensive than the old

Trailing cucumbers

Bush cucumbers

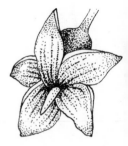

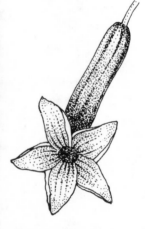

Cucumber flowers

kinds, but well worth the extra. There are also some new varieties developed in Japan which are very long and thin and have extremely juicy flesh, as well as the pickling varieties.

Soil and manuring
Since cucumbers are tender plants, they need the warmest spot possible. Being nearly all water (over 95%), they are very thirsty plants and need rich, moist soil with as much organic matter in it as possible. If you can dig in plenty of manure or compost, that is the ideal. If not, use peat, hop-manure, leaf mold or similar material. Enrich the soil in this way to at least 12 inches down, so as to encourage a vigorous growth of deep, moisture-seeking roots.

Stopping laterals

Sowing

If you live in the Pacific Northwest, in fog belt areas, the Rocky Mountain states and in other localities with a limited growing season, start your seedlings off under glass so that they have made sturdy young plants by planting-out time. With a greenhouse or cold frame you can sow in mid to late spring in 3-inch pots of seed mix; do not sow before this, or the plants will be pot-bound when the time comes to put them out.

Without such facilities, you may have to wait a little longer and sow direct into the soil. Even then you can gain a week or two by sowing in late spring and covering with a plastic cap or glass jar. If you have no such protection to give, wait until early summer. In each case, whether sowing in a pot or direct into the ground, plant the seeds point downwards, an inch or so below the surface and give a thorough watering. With pots, sow a single seed in each (but a few more than you need, in case some do not germinate), and with sowing direct into the soil, put the seeds in groups of three, to be thinned later so as to leave only the strongest.

Planting

Plants raised in pots—either by yourself or bought from a nurseryman—should not be planted in the open until danger of frost is past. It is very important not to damage the roots, or they may rot. A good way to avoid this is to plant an empty pot up to its rim, firm the soil round it, lift the pot out again, and there you have a hole that will exactly fit the roots of the plant after you have gently knocked it out of the pot in which it has been growing. Finish by giving each plant a good drink of water.

Care during growth

Keep the plants weeded and watered at all times. When a plant has made seven or eight leaves, pinch out the growing tip. New shoots will appear, and these can be trained either along the ground or up stout sticks or netting.

Cucumber flowers, as pictured here, are of two kinds: the one on a plain stalk is a male, and the one with the tiny fruit behind the flower is a female. It is from these females that the cucumbers will develop. To keep the plants within bounds, and to concentrate the plant's energy into swelling the fruits as quickly as possible, many growers stop side shoots (i.e., pick off the growing point) at two leaves beyond the female flower with its developing baby cucumber, as shown. Any side shoots that do not produce any fruits at all should have the growing tip pinched out after the seventh leaf.

When the plants have started bearing good size fruit, they will crop all the better if they are given some fertilizer every ten days or so. To prevent fruit from getting muddy, place a tile under it—or failing that a layer of straw.

Gathering

Start cutting the cucumbers as soon as they reach a usable size. Do not leave them on the plant to see how big they can grow, because that will only make them get tough; besides, the regular cutting of young fruit will cause more to grow. In this way you should get a constant supply of cucumbers until the fall frosts kill the plants.

Pests and diseases

CUCUMBER BEETLE The striped cucumber beetle in the east, and the spotted in the west are basically the same bug and can eat most parts of the plant unless controlled by rotenone.

RED SPIDER MITE If leaves turn pale, sickly and lacking in vigor, as pictured here, they are the victims of red spider mite. This tiny creature, which can only be seen under a magnifying glass, sucks out the sap, enfeebles the whole plant and reduces the crop. It is never so bad outdoors as under glass, but in dry conditions it can do great damage.

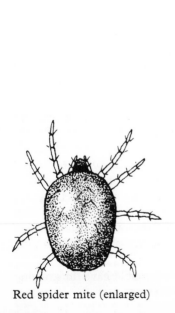

Red spider mite (enlarged)

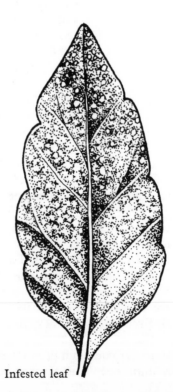

Infested leaf

Foot rot

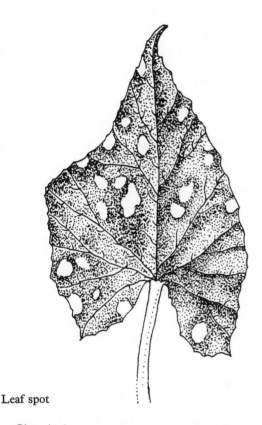

Leaf spot

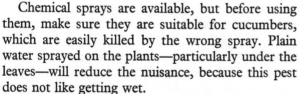

Withering fruit

Chemical sprays are available, but before using them, make sure they are suitable for cucumbers, which are easily killed by the wrong spray. Plain water sprayed on the plants—particularly under the leaves—will reduce the nuisance, because this pest does not like getting wet.

FOOT ROT As shown, this causes the stem to wither at the base, and the whole plant collapses. The trouble is encouraged by wet conditions and can be controlled by setting the plants on mounds of soil (as shown under squashes) so that water runs off instead of remaining around the base of the stem.

LEAF SPOT This disease, pictured here, can cause considerable trouble under glass but is rarely serious outdoors. Pick off affected leaves and remove them.

WITHERING FRUITS It is very annoying when a promising young fruit, instead of swelling, withers from the flower end, as shown here. This is usually caused outdoors by dry conditions and can be remedied by spraying the plants with plain water in the evening during hot weather.

SQUASHES AND ZUCCHINI

There is really no botanical difference between these vegetables, which are nothing but garden varieties of the same species, *Cucurbita pepo*, a relative of the cucumber. As with the cucumber, nobody knows where it originated in the wild. It is thought to have been a native of some part of South America. During the four centuries or so that the species has been cultivated, gardeners and plant breeders have developed it into a number of strikingly different forms—so different that it is difficult for a non-botanist to recognize that they are merely varieties of the same thing.

From the vegetable-grower's point of view, there are two distinct types.

SUMMER SQUASH that can be grown throughout the country and take around two months to grow from seed to maturity.

Amount of seed required
A small packet will give more than enough plants for normal needs.

When to sow
Mid to late spring under glass. Early summer outdoors.

Depth to sow
1 in. (c. 2.5 cm.).

When to plant
June.

Distance between plants
Bush varieties, 30 in. (c. 75 cm.).
Trailing varieties, 4 ft. (c. 1.20 m.).

Seedlings appear
Within 7–10 days.

Ready to cut
Mid to late summer onwards.

WINTER SQUASH that take around four months to ripen and need more growing space devoted to their cultivation than the summer varieties. They are not well suited to hot, arid parts of the country. The fruits have hard shells and store well for use throughout the winter.

ZUCCHINI are varieties of summer squash with a very compact habit of growth and from which the immature fruits are cut over a period of many weeks while they are soft and still not much bigger than a cigar. It is very important that the fruits should be cut regularly during the summer while they are small, so as to encourage the formation of as many more as possible for the longest possible time. There are green-skinned zucchini and now the newer golden-skinned ones which, though slightly tougher, have great eye-appeal and keep their sunshine color even when cooked.

Most of the summer squash are bush varieties, but winter squash may be trailing (sometimes referred to as running or vine types). While the trailing sorts are more prolific they ramble all over the ground and are hard to keep under control, though you can grow them upwards on a 'wigwam' of stakes, crossing each other at the top and fixed together as shown. However, unless you have a great deal of space to spare, it is better not to grow the trailing sorts of squash, which grow at a tremendous rate and need constant cutting and training to prevent them from overwhelming neighboring plants. The bush kinds are more compact, take up less room and are easier to tame.

There are now some F1 hybrids which give a very large crop and make no sideshoots at all; the plant grows upwards, almost like a small shrub, but needs no support and produces its fruit in successive layers for several months.

Zucchini

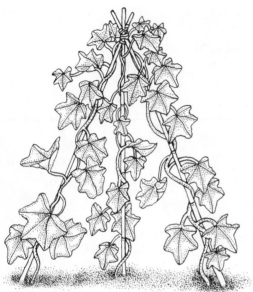

Supporting trailing squash

Care during growth
Same as for *Cucumbers*.

FERTILIZING THE FLOWERS As with cucumbers, male and female flowers are different in their structure, the female having a small fruit behind them and the male not, as pictured. Unlike cucumbers, which set plenty of fruit without help, squash are more likely to give a good crop if you pollinate them. Simply pick a male flower when it has opened and produced plenty of yellow pollen grains and stick into the heart of a female flower so that the pollen adheres. This will bring about sexual fusion and cause the embryo fruit to swell and develop.

VEGETABLE SPAGHETTI is a novelty type of squash that grows very quickly and produces creamy-orange colored fruits which should be cut when they are 8 inches long. If they are boiled for twenty minutes and then cut open, the inside can be scooped out, seasoned and eaten just like spaghetti.

Soil, manuring, sowing and planting
Exactly the same as for *Cucumbers*.

Since the soft stem is easily rotted at the base if it is allowed to stand in water, many good growers plant squash in raised mounds of earth, as shown, so that water can run off and drain away.

Planting seedlings on mound

Zucchini flowers

unlikely to keep for very long.

Pests and diseases
Same as for *Cucumbers*.

SQUASH VINE BORER can be prevented by spraying the leaves with malathion. If the borers have already entered the stem carefully slit the stem with a sharp knife to remove and destroy the bugs.

SQUASH BUGS can be destroyed by rotenone or pick off the brown egg clusters by hand.

PUMPKINS
If you have a considerable amount of space, one or two pumpkin plants will produce some very large fruit to make into pumpkin pie during the fall and to store for use during the winter. The pumpkin is grown in exactly the same way as squash, and needs the same kind of soil and treatment. It is thought by many to be rather hardier, and the fruits, with their tough skin which can become as hard as wood, are often left out in the open longer than other members of their family, to ripen thoroughly before being cut and put into store. While they are outside, stand the fruit on a strong tile or piece of wood to prevent it from being ruined by mud.

Pests and diseases
The same sorts of troubles can occur to the pumpkin as to the other members of the family, but not usually to the same extent, because the pumpkin seems to have a rather more rugged constitution and to be less attractive to pests.

Gathering
Same as for *Cucumbers*.

When you are going to use the fruit young and fresh, always cut it before it reaches full size. That is particularly important with zucchini, which should be eaten while they are still babies. In that way, not only will the fruits be much more tender, tastier and juicier, but the plant will be stimulated into producing more fruit.

On the other hand, if you want to store any squashes for the winter, wait until the skin has become a hard rind before you cut the fruit. Then it will keep well if stored in a cool, dry, frost-proof place. Fruit cut before its skin has hardened is

27. Sweet corn

This popular vegetable is a very strange form of grass. Since it is never found in the wild, nobody knows exactly where it originated, but it was a food crop in Mexico and neighboring territories long before the exploration and settlement of the New World.

In the Southern States, corn is easy to grow and can be sown without risk early in the spring. Further north it becomes more difficult, because it is easily damaged by cold weather, so that sowing has to be delayed until the danger of severe frosts is over. That in turn used to bring problems, because the plant had to grow very tall and produce a large number of leaves before it was able to start making cobs at all. And because it did its growing at night, it needed long nights for fast growth. But in places liable to frost, long nights, being early in the year, are cold nights. So if to get quick growth the corn was sown early, it would most likely be killed by frost. If, on the other hand, it was sown later, the nights were too short for good growth and the plants could not grow tall enough to produce cobs before the autumn frosts destroyed them.

Now the difficulty has vanished. Over the past few years plant breeders have produced varieties of corn that do not grow tall and do not have to form many leaves before they can develop cobs. They are also hardier, and most of them are F1 hybrids, which give more reliable and uniform results. In colder regions, then, choose one of these and, if the weather is reasonable, you will be able to pick your own excellent cobs of corn.

Soil and manuring

Choose a spot sheltered from the wind if possible. Do not use freshly manured ground or the plants will make a great deal of leaf growth at the expense of producing cobs. Use ground well manured for a previous crop, or else dig in plenty of compost. Give the soil a sprinkling of general fertilizer a few days before sowing.

Sowing

Do not sow until the danger of frost is over. Plant the seeds in pairs, 18 inches apart from the next pair each way. Do not sow in a single row but in a block at least three plants long and three wide. If you have some cloches you can put them over the plants for two or three weeks for protection, but this is not really necessary except in cold or windy conditions.

Care during growth

Weed the plants as they come up, and thin each pair of seedlings to leave only the stronger one.

SUPPORTING The plants will not need staking, but earthing-up three or four inches high round the base of the stem will give support in high winds.

WATERING In the early stages the young plants may need watering to prevent them from wilting. A mulch of compost or leaf mould after watering

Amount of seed required
½ oz. (c. 15 g.) will sow 30 ft. (c. 9 m.).

When to sow
Spring.

Depth to sow
1 in. (c. 2.5 cm.).

Distance between plants
18 in. (c. 45 cm.) each way.

Shoots appear
In about a week.

Ready for picking
Late summer onwards.

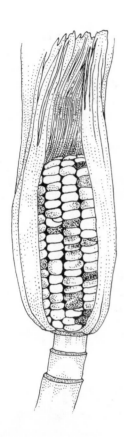

Grain rot

Sweet corn

will keep in the moisture.

Habit of growth

When the plants are nearing their full height, they will send up loose spikes of male flowers at the top. Lower down the stem silky tassels will appear; these are the female parts, and pollen falling on them from the male flowers above will cause the cobs to swell and ripen. The reason for planting in blocks and not in lines is to ensure that the pollen is not simply blown away but falls on the tassels where it is needed.

Gathering

After pollination, the tassels will wither. A few weeks later the cobs will be ripe and can be cut or snapped off the plants. Gather while the seeds are still soft and juicy.

Pests and diseases

GRAIN ROT This disease, as pictured, turns infected seeds moldy. Remove affected plants.

SMUT This fungus turns cobs swollen and distorted. Remove them and burn infected plants.

EUROPEAN CORN BORERS Spray or dust with sevin.

28. Herbs

MOST vegetable gardeners grow a few plants of parsley, and perhaps a clump of mint or thyme, but for some reason they stop there. When they need any other herbs for cooking they have to buy them in packets, dried. But dried herbs are only ghosts of themselves. You have never tasted their real flavor until you have had them freshly picked, preferably from your own garden, and you can, of course, dry your own herbs for use in the winter, as well as using them fresh during the growing season.

One of the great virtues of herbs, apart from the exciting flavors they give to food and their medicinal properties (real or imagined), is that they will grow readily in ground that is not much good for anything else. Most of them are best in rather poor, dry soil. Not only will that stop them from growing so vigorously that they crowd each other and invade parts of the garden where they are not wanted, but it will actually improve their flavour. The drier the soil, the less sap there is in the plant; the less sap there

is, the more concentrated it becomes; and the more concentrated it becomes, the stronger and more pronounced the flavor. It is a good idea to grow herbs beside a path, so that you can gather them at the last moment, just when they are wanted for cooking, without getting your feet dirty. There are so many different herbs that it is only possible to give a selection here of the most readily available and useful ones. To make the list as practical as possible, they have been divided into three groups; perennials, hardy annuals, and half-hardy annuals.

Perennials

This group consists of herbs that stay in the ground from year to year and are hardy enough to survive most winters without any protection. Included here are both the herbaceous kinds, which die right down to the ground during the winter and sprout again in the spring, and the shrubs and sub-shrubs, which remain alive and give pickings of leaves in winter.

Chives

Mint

BAY (*Laurus nobilis*)
This evergreen provides the bay leaves used in cooking. It can be planted in the open ground but becomes rather big. A neat specimen bought in a large pot or tub will keep within bounds, and can be brought inside if extra-cold weather threatens.

CHIVES (*Allium schoenoprasum*)
This relative of the onion, pictured here, forms clumps of small bulbs with grass-like foliage that can be chopped to give a mild flavor of onions to salads, sandwiches, soups, sauces etc. It dies down during winter, but gives pickings most of the year. It may be grown from seed sown in spring, but better results are usually obtained by buying plants of proved varieties. Set the plants, 6 inches apart, where it is easy to get at them for picking.

FENNEL (*Foeniculum vulgare*)
The very decorative leaves are used to flavor sauces, pickles, fish, meat and vegetable dishes and salads. They also make a striking addition to flower-arrangements. There is a bronze-leaved kind which is particularly handsome. Fennel dies down during the winter and can be grown from seed sown in spring or from bought plants.

MINT (*Mentha species*)
This well-known flavoring for sauces, vegetables (especially peas) and cooling drinks is such a rampant grower that it can become a nuisance. The thrusting underground stems, or stolons, shown here, will invade other plants' territory if given a chance. Give it a patch to itself, or if that is not possible sink an old bucket with the bottom knocked out in the ground and plant the mint in that so that the roots cannot spread sideways. There are many

Mint roots

varieties of mint, all of which die down during winter. A disease called Mint Rust sometimes attacks the ordinary smooth-leaved mint causing dark patches, as shown, which can be very destructive. The best way to avoid it is to grow the round-leaved hairy species called Apple-mint (*Mentha rotundifolia*) which is immune to rust and many people think has a better flavor.

OREGANO (*Origanum vulgare*)
A key ingredient in the best made pizza, and also widely used with tomatoes and mushrooms, in salad dressings and with many vegetables and meats.

Mint rust

Raise oregano from seeds sown indoors in the spring. Transplant when 3 inches high to a well-drained, sunny place. Replant every three years.

ROSEMARY (*Rosmarinus officinalis*)
This small shrub has very pungent, narrow, evergreen leaves. A sprig stuck into chicken or meat before roasting and fished out before serving brings it to life. Rosemary can be raised from seed sown in spring but is much better grown from a rooted cutting of a good variety, either bought or taken from a friend's plant.

SAGE (*Salvia officinalis*)
The leaves of this well-known shrub are an indispensable ingredient of stuffing to accompany rich meats such as pork, duck and goose. It will grow anywhere, and spreads so much that new plants should be raised from cuttings every few years and the old ones thrown away. Sage grows easily from seed, but it is much better to buy plants of a good

variety. There is a highly desirable kind that never flowers and grows in a much neater and more compact way than the usual sort.

TARRAGON (*Artemisia dracunculus*)
The chopped-up leaves of this member of the daisy family make all the difference to egg and poultry dishes, sauces and soups, and lift mixed salads onto a higher plane. Tarragon dies down during the winter and can be propagated during that time from pieces of root cut off and planted. It can also be raised from seed in the spring but is best bought as plants of a good variety. In hard frost, protect plants with a covering of straw or sand.

THYME (*Thymus vulgaris*)
This creeping evergreen, known as Common Thyme, and by botanists a sub-shrub, is not only essential to the cook's bouquet garni, but is used to enliven so many dishes that it is impossible to mention them all. It will grow almost anywhere and can be raised

Thyme

Parsley

Sage

Fennel

from seed sown in spring, but you would be much better advised to obtain plants of a good variety. There is another species, the Lemon Thyme (*Thymus x citriodorus*), which is preferred by some cooks; it is less pungent and has a distinct scent of lemons.

WINTER SAVORY (*Satureja montana*)
This low-growing sub-shrub has leaves which can be picked fresh all the winter and have a delightful aroma like mixed herbs.

Hardy annuals
This groups contains the herbs which can be sown outside in spring without protection and will not be injured by normal frosts. All can be sown either in a shallow drill where they are to remain or in pots of soil or seed compost to be planted out later.

CHERVIL (*Anthriscus cerefolium*)
The chopped leaves add a tang to fish dishes, omelets and salads.

Marjoram

CORIANDER (*Coriandrum sativum*)
During growth this herb has a disgusting smell, described by some as like bed-bugs and others as like rubber. But when the seeds are gathered and ripened they develop a delightful aroma which adds life to many dishes.

DILL (*Anethum graveolens*)
The leaves and seeds are both used in fish and cheese dishes, and added to vinegar to make dill pickle.

PARSLEY (*Petroselinum crispum*)
This, the most widely used of all herbs in cookery, will grow almost anywhere but prefers moderately good soil.

It is sown in early spring for summer and fall use and in mid summer for winter and spring. Do not worry if the seed does not come up for several weeks; it often takes a long time to germinate. Though not strictly an annual, parsley is best treated as such, because old plants get straggly and coarse and are best disposed of on the compost heap.

Half-hardy annuals
Being more likely to be damaged by cold than the previous group, these should not be sown in the open ground until late spring.

BASIL (*Ocimum basilicum*)
This is probably the spiciest herb that can be grown in the open in temperate climates. If frost threatens after it has come up, protect it temporarily at night with an upside-down flower pot or glass jar over it.

SWEET MARJORAM (*Marjorana hortensis*)
The very sweet-scented leaves of this herb are used in many dishes: soups, stews, sauces and very sparingly in salads. It is grown as an annual where winters are freezing, and as a perennial in warmer parts.

29. Rhubarb

IF YOU HAVE space to grow it—and it does take up a good deal of room if you grow it properly—you should always have a few plants of rhubarb in your vegetable patch. Rhubarb gives you the earliest taste of fresh fruit in the year, just when you are becoming bored with canned and frozen stuff. Rhubarb is one of the very few commonly cultivated members of the dock family, a family best known for burdening the gardener's life with some of the most heart-breaking and back-breaking weeds.

Coming as it does from Siberia, it will put up with Arctic weather; yet although it comes cheerfully through the most intense cold, it does not seem to suffer from heat either. Its huge leaves shade the base of the plant from the sun's rays and keep the ground moist beneath them. The reason for the sharp, fruity taste of rhubarb is that its stalks contain a certain amount of acid. Never, never try to eat any part of the green leaves. These green parts contain such a high concentration of oxalic acid that they are deadly poisonous; many people have killed themselves by trying to eat rhubarb leaves as a green vegetable.

Sowing

It is much better to buy roots than to raise them from seed. Even the most carefully selected seed from the best plant will produce a varied assortment of offspring, most of them inferior in quality to their parent. However, seed is cheaper than roots, so you may wish to try it.

The best time to sow is early to mid spring. Choose rich soil in a spot that will not be needed until next year. Sow the seed very thinly in a drill ½ inch deep.

When the seedlings appear thin them to 6 inches apart and leave them until the winter, when they will be ready for transplanting.

Soil and manuring

Rhubarb will remain in position for a good many years, so it is best planted at the end of your plot, or better still in a separate place, where it will not interfere with cultivation and the rotation of crops. Choose really deep, rich soil and incorporate plenty of manure or compost below the topsoil. A week or two before planting, apply a general fertilizer to the surface and rake it in.

Rhubarb

Planting

Bought roots are usually best because they are not untried seedlings but actually portions split from a known variety of proved and superior performance. However, whether you buy roots or raise plants yourself from seed, they should be planted in their permanent quarters either in late fall or in early spring. Dig planting holes 3 feet apart and deep enough to take all the roots and leave the tops just peeping out of the soil. Tread the soil firmly round the plants and water them well in so as to settle the soil around the roots.

Care during growth

All that is needed is to remove weeds during the growing season. A dressing of general fertilizer in early to mid summer will give growth a boost, but do not apply fertilizer later than that or it may cause soft fall growth which could be damaged by frost.

Picking

Do not pick any stalks the first year; let the plants build up their strength. In subsequent years pick stalks when they are ready, by holding them as low as possible and pulling them off with a slight twist. Do not pick all the leaves off any plant or you will seriously weaken it; always leave three or four.

Forcing

To get very early pickings, cover the crowns of one or two plants in early winter with a large pot or bucket, upside-down, as shown. Cover that with straw or leaves, if possible, to give more warmth. In late winter, young forced stalks should be fit to pick.

Stop picking by mid summer and let the leaves develop to build up the plant's strength. Sprinkle fertilizer round the base, and mulch with a layer of compost, leaf-mold or damp peat.

Cut out any flower-stalks as soon as they appear or they will sap the plant's energy.

Pests and diseases

Hardly anything troubles rhubarb, but the following disease can cause problems.

CROWN ROT   As pictured, this eats away the crown, causing a blackened cavity. There is no effective cure. Remove affected plants and burn them.

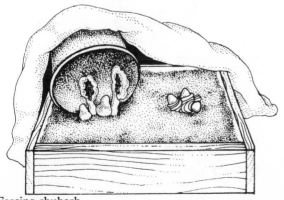

Forcing rhubarb

Crown rot

30. Asparagus

AN EXPENSIVE luxury in the stores, this delicious vegetable is perhaps the cheapest of all to grow yourself, because the same plants go on producing crops year after year. Asparagus will grow well throughout most of the country except the Gulf States.

Asparagus is usually grown from 'crowns' bought from a nursery. It can also be raised from seed. This is cheaper but slower, so you have to wait a year or two longer before you can start eating the results, and seeds can produce very mixed plants, some good and some not so good.

There is also a certain problem about sex, but we will come to that later.

Sowing
This is done in a seed-bed, in mid spring. Rake a little general fertilizer into the soil, then draw a drill ½ inch deep. Sow the seed thinly along this, cover with soil, tread firm and rake smooth. Keep the bed weeded, and thin the seedlings as they grow. By the end of the growing season they should be 5 or 6 inches apart. Then their roots will not be tangled together when the time comes to transplant them next spring.

Soil and manuring
The asparagus bed is going to stay in the same place for a good many years, so it must not interfere with the crop rotation of your other vegetables. The best thing is to give it a patch all to itself.

The soil must be well drained, because asparagus cannot bear to have its roots in water. If necessary, use methods such as those described in the section *Improving the soil*.

The ground must also be rich in organic matter, so mix plenty of manure or compost into the second spit. Do this during *double-digging*, which is an essential operation in preparing a good asparagus bed.

Amount of seed required
½ oz. (c. 15 g.) will produce hundreds of plants.

When to sow
Early to mid spring.

Depth to sow
½ in. (c. 1 cm.).

Shoots appear
Within 2 weeks.

When to plant
Mid spring (earlier in mild-winter areas).

Distance apart of plants
18 in. (c. 45 cm.).

Distance between rows
3 ft. (c. 90 cm.).

Ready to cut
2 years after planting, then every year.

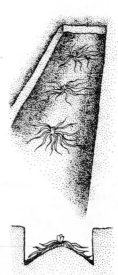

Planting (See p. 148)

Asparagus bed

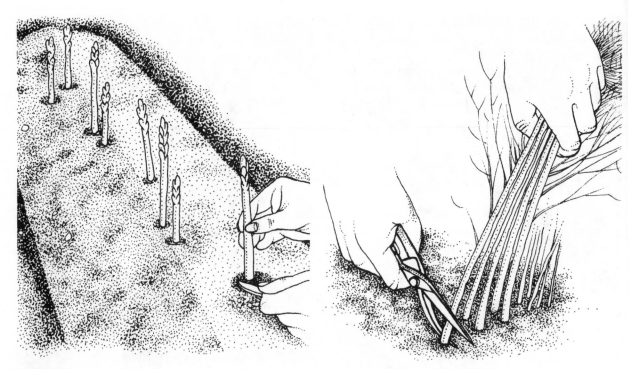

Cutting asparagus

Removing foliage

Planting

This is best done in mid spring, whether you raise your own plants from seed or buy them. The soil will be warming up by then, giving the roots a welcome and encouraging them to grow.

Asparagus has separate male and female plants. Experts say that the male ones are superior, and that therefore your bed should contain males only. The snag is that you cannot tell a seedling's sex until it is two or three years old, by which time it hates being transplanted. So forget about sex discrimination and plant one-year olds, which are cheaper anyway.

Dig planting trenches 12 inches wide, 9 inches deep and 3 feet apart (if you have plenty of space, make that 4 feet apart). Replace some of the soil to make a ridge along the middle of the trench. Then, as shown, you can seat the crowns on this ridge with their roots spread out on each side. Cover them with soil, make it firm, and give a thorough watering.

Cutting

Do not cut any spears the first year after planting. In subsequent years start cutting spears when they reach 4 or 5 inches high, slicing them off cleanly with a knife 3 inches below ground level, as shown. Continue cutting for six weeks, then stop. After that, spears must be allowed to grow to their full height. In the fall, when the tops turn yellow, cut them off an inch or two above ground level, as pictured here.

Each spring give a dressing of complete fertilizer between the rows and mulch the surface with a good layer of compost or leaf mold.

Pests and diseases

One serious pest may attack asparagus, but disease is mercifully rare, provided you select one of the Washington varieties, bred with a resistance to rust.

ASPARAGUS BEETLE This, as shown, or its twelve-spotted relative, can damage the plants quite severely by its nibbling. Sprays are available, but picking off the pests and destroying them is effective.

FROST DAMAGE If tips shrink and wither as in the picture, they have been damaged by frost. Some protection can be given by covering the bed with straw, compost or leaves when severe weather threatens.

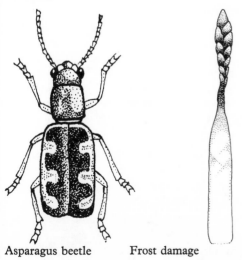

Asparagus beetle   Frost damage

Feeding

This is a very important annual routine if you want your asparagus bed to go on producing good crops. Asparagus is a very heavy feeder and takes a large amount of nourishment from the soil. If you continue to cut and remove young spears year after year without replacing that nourishment, the plants are bound to become weaker, and instead of growing fat and juicy the spears will become thin and hard. As with all permanent crops, it is particularly important to remove weeds as soon as they appear; otherwise within a year or two the asparagus bed will become a tangle of the nastiest perennial menaces such as bindweed and quackgrass, which not only look unsightly and make cultivation difficult but rob the soil of the plant foods that the asparagus so hungrily needs. Many growers give the asparagus bed a dressing of common salt (sodium chloride) each spring and say that it stimulates growth. Others deny this and point out that excellent crops of asparagus can be grown without any salt at all. The truth of the matter seems to be that since asparagus grows wild in salty places near the sea it can put up with more salt than most other plants can. So salt on the asparagus bed seems to act as a kind of selective weedkiller, discouraging the weeds but not the asparagus.

31. Artichokes

MANY LOVERS of good food believe that this name should only be applied to that delicious vegetable the Globe Artichoke (*Cynara scolymus*), which originally came from the Mediterranean region—though nobody can now find it growing wild anywhere—and of which the part that is eaten is the flower head. Others use the name also for a quite different species, the Jerusalem Artichoke (*Helianthus tuberosus*), which is also called Girasole or the American artichoke, of which the part that is eaten is the underground tubers.

They are so different that we will deal with them separately.

GLOBE ARTICHOKE
This is almost the only member of the thistle family to be eaten by human beings. (Its close relative the Cardoon, dealt with briefly below, is occasionally eaten too.) It can be raised from seed, but is usually grown from offshoots or divisions of named varieties.

Amount of seed required
One small packet will give more plants than you can use.

When to sow
Early to mid spring.

Depth to sow
½ in. (c. 1 cm.).

Seedlings appear
Within 14 days.

When to plant
Mid spring.

Distance between plants
30 in. (c. 75 cm.).

Ready to cut
Early summer onwards.

Sowing
Plants raised from seed are likely to be variable and unlikely to yield the best flower heads. If, however, you want to try sowing, wait until the ground feels warm and there is no danger of hard frosts. Sow in a place that will not be needed for anything else until next spring, when the seedlings will be ready for transplanting. Sow thinly in a drill ½ inch deep. Thin out seedlings to 12 inches apart.

Planting
In mid or late spring, the resulting seedlings may be planted in their permanent quarters, or you can use plants of a tried and proved variety. These are usually propagated by side shoots, or 'suckers', which appear at the base of old plants, as shown. Several of these appear every year, so once you have your first plant you will never need to buy any more. Plant firmly, 30 inches apart, and water the plants well in. Do not worry if they droop at first; they will soon pick up as they grow new roots.

Soil and manuring
As the plants are going to remain in the same place

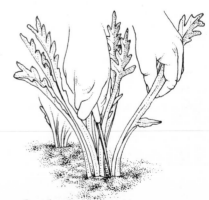

Side shoots for planting

for several years, the soil should be as rich as possible, with plenty of manure or compost dug in, and a dressing of general fertilizer applied to the surface before planting.

Care during growth
Keep the artichoke bed weeded and water the plants when young in dry weather to prevent drooping. It is a very good idea to mulch the soil round the plants with a good layer of compost or leaf mold. This will keep the plants vigorous, and smother most weeds and make those that do appear easier to pull out. When the flower heads start forming, remove side buds, leaving the center one on the stem to swell into a good size head.

Cutting
As the flower heads reach a good size cut them while they are still green and fleshy. Do not leave them to get hard.

Winter protection
In very cold weather, some people protect the plants by putting straw, bracken or similar material over the crowns. This should not be necessary if you allowed the old tops to remain on the plants instead of cutting them off in the fall. Old tops may not look very tidy, but they are the frost protection provided by nature.

CARDOON
This close relation of the globe artichoke is grown from seed sown in mid spring, planted in trenches and earthed-up just like *Celery*. It is the blanched leaf stalks that are eaten, not the flower-heads.

GIRASOLE, OR THE JERUSALEM ARTICHOKE
This vegetable is a kind of sunflower grown for its tubers, which are like knobbly potatoes but do not contain starch. Plant tubers in good, well dug soil in early spring, 2 feet apart. The plants will grow to about 6 feet tall. Leave the tubers in the ground and dig them as required during the winter after the tops have withered. Search thoroughly for the tubers as they grow at the end of an extensive root system and may easily be overlooked.

Globe artichoke

32. Vegetable protein

UNTIL quite recently a great many people believed that there was one vital foodstuff which could not be produced effectively from the vegetable garden. That foodstuff was protein, the substance from which each one of us started and which forms the building-blocks of our whole body.

We cannot do without protein in our daily diet, and for most of us the main source of that protein up to now has been meat. Even vegetarians have relied principally on animal products, such as milk, eggs and cheese, for this essential requirement.

Now, with meat and all the other animal products becoming scarcer and more expensive all the time, some people are beginning to question whether we really do need to be so dependent on such things. After all, every scrap of protein we eat has been produced by plants in the first place. Animals are merely rather inefficient factories for processing that vegetable protein into other forms, losing as they do a large part of its goodness in such energy-wasting activities as chewing, breathing and moving about.

Can we obtain our protein direct from plants, without the wasteful and expensive process of passing it through animals first? The answer is that we can, if we grow the right things and if we allow them to ripen their seeds. A fully mature seed is a package of concentrated goodness, filled with all the protein and other food substances intended to give the embryo plant inside it the best possible start in life.

However, because most of us have got into the habit of eating our seed vegetables, such as peas and beans, as an accompaniment to other protein—usually meat—we eat them young, before they have developed their own protein power. If instead you allow pods of peas, snap, and other beans to ripen fully and store the dried seeds you will find that when soaked and cooked they provide an excellent and tasty source of protein.

Other kinds, bred not to be eaten green at all but only as ripe seeds, provide an even richer source. The following is a selection of some of these high-protein vegetables, for attractive and nourishing meatless dishes.

SOYBEANS

Long recognized as perhaps the most protein-rich food in the world, and containing 40 per cent protein compared with 25 per cent in beef-steak, soybeans are native to the Far East. Until recently they were only thought suitable for growing in hot climates. Now, revolutionary new varieties have been developed which will thrive in all our gardens. The seeds are smaller than ordinary beans; as little as one ounce will sow a row 40 feet long. Sow in rather dry ground in late spring or early summer when the danger of frost is over. Make drills 2 inches deep and 9 inches apart, and sow the seeds about 3 inches apart along these.

The plants will grow no higher than 2 feet. The purple flowers are very small and do not open fully, so you may well not notice that the plants have flowered at all until one day you see that bunches of small, hairy pods are forming. Leave them until the leaves go yellow and the pods turn rusty brown, then pull up the plants and let them dry for a few days so that the pods become brittle and papery. Shell out the beans, of which there will be only three or four in a pod, and leave them for a few more days to dry before storing them.

GARBANZO

Garbanzo, or chickpea plants, produce small pods usually with one seed per pod. They can be cultivated like bush beans and after the pods ripen the beans can be dried and prepared by boiling or roasting.

HARICOT BEANS
Different varieties have different colored seeds—white, cream and brown. They make dwarf plants and should be sown 6 inches apart in rows 2 feet apart in late spring.

HULLED PUMPKIN SEEDS
These taste like nuts, contain 30 per cent protein and need no shelling. Grow exactly like *Pumpkins* but allow the fruits to ripen to a deep orange color; then cut them open and scoop out the seeds. Wash these and dry them. Eaten raw, they make a tasty cocktail snack.

Beans—the high protein vegetable

33. Sprouting seeds

WHETHER you have a vegetable garden or not, you can grow delicious fresh produce all the year round in your kitchen or a cupboard, or even the bathroom. What is more, it is produce packed with more concentrated goodness than you could get from any other source.

All you need is a packet of seed, a glass jar, a small piece of cheesecloth and an elastic band.

As we saw in the previous section *Vegetable protein*, seeds are packages of stored nourishment ready to feed the baby plants during their helpless early days before they are able to feed themselves from the soil, the air and the sunlight. As soon as the seeds begin to sprout, they undergo a transformation. In addition to protein, carbohydrates and other stored food they rapidly develop quantities of vitamins and other life-substances to force the seedlings into growth. By the time the seeds have sprouted for a few days they are powerhouses of growth and health.

The easiest way to sprout seed is to put some in a glass jar (not too much, because it is going to swell many times its present bulk), stretch a piece of cheesecloth across the mouth of the jar and fix it in place with an elastic band. Fill the jar with water, shake vigorously so that each seed is wet all over, then empty out the water and lay the jar on its side in a warm place. Fill the jar with water and empty it out again every morning and evening. Sprouts will appear from the seeds and will be big enough to use (2 or 3 inches long) within 3 to 9 days according to the kind of seed used.

As with most of the vegetables mentioned in the previous section, *Vegetable protein*, the most important for our purpose are members of the pea and bean family, known as leguminous plants. These, as explained in the section *Peas and beans*, have the ability to take nitrogen from the air and so are a very rich source of this element, which is a vital constituent of protein.

Only buy seeds for sprouting from a health food store as seeds for growing are often coated with chemicals. Use fresh and crisp in salads; they are particularly welcome during the winter when there is very little other fresh salad about. Or the sprouts make a delicious and nourishing ingredient in stews and other cooked dishes.

There are also some leguminous species that are particularly suitable for sprouting, and seed of these is sold by some of the better-class seedsmen. The following is a selection of some of these special sprouting kinds.

ALFALFA

For many years this has been grown as a valuable forage crop for cattle. Recently, it has been found to be excellent for sprouting for salads, nearly as high in protein as soya, rich in all the vitamins and as tasty as fresh garden peas.

ADZUKI BEANS

This close relative of the *Rice Bean*, a vitally important source of protein in China and Japan, has been cultivated for centuries for its outstanding food value. Its red seeds and white sprouts look particularly attractive and it has an appealing nutty taste.

FENUGREEK

The piquant spicy flavour of this rich source of protein and vitamins, said to be a great defender against the common cold, makes the sprouts specially suitable in curries and soups.

MUNG BEAN

This is the well-known Chinese Sprouting Bean,

one of the most important ingredients used in Chinese cookery. It is commonly eaten cooked until soft, but is also attractive and highly nutritious eaten raw and crisp in sandwiches and salads.

LENTILS

For many years we have used lentils in soups and other dishes as a combined protein provider and thickener. Now it has been found that sprouted lentils have even more food value together with a flavor not unlike hazelnuts. Try sprouted lentils added to lentil soup; the contrast between the smoothness of the soup and the crunchiness of the sprouts makes very pleasant eating.

Seeds sprouted in a jar

Index